THE COMPLETE IDIOT'S GUIDE® TO

Crochet Projects

Illustrated

by Marcy Smith

ALPHA
A member of Penguin Group (USA) Inc.

mjwn

ALPHA BOOKS

Published by the Penguin Group

Penguin Group (USA) Inc., 375 Hudson Street, New York, New York 10014, USA

Penguin Group (Canada), 90 Eglinton Avenue East, Suite 700, Toronto, Ontario M4P 2Y3, Canada (a division of Pearson Penguin Canada Inc.)

Penguin Books Ltd., 80 Strand, London WC2R 0RL, England

Penguin Ireland, 25 St. Stephen's Green, Dublin 2, Ireland (a division of Penguin Books Ltd.)

Penguin Group (Australia), 250 Camberwell Road, Camberwell, Victoria 3124, Australia (a division of Pearson Australia Group Pty. Ltd.)

Penguin Books India Pvt. Ltd., 11 Community Centre, Panchsheel Park, New Delhi—110 017, India

Penguin Group (NZ), 67 Apollo Drive, Rosedale, North Shore, Auckland 1311, New Zealand (a division of Pearson New Zealand Ltd.)

Penguin Books (South Africa) (Pty.) Ltd., 24 Sturdee Avenue, Rosebank, Johannesburg 2196, South Africa

Penguin Books Ltd., Registered Offices: 80 Strand, London WC2R 0RL, England

International Standard Book Number: 978-1-59257-618-0
Library of Congress Catalog Card Number: 2007928978

09   08   07   8   7   6   5   4   3   2   1

Interpretation of the printing code: The rightmost number of the first series of numbers is the year of the book's printing; the rightmost number of the second series of numbers is the number of the book's printing. For example, a printing code of 07-1 shows that the first printing occurred in 2007.

Printed in the United States of America

Note: This publication contains the opinions and ideas of its author. It is intended to provide helpful and informative material on the subject matter covered. It is sold with the understanding that the author and publisher are not engaged in rendering professional services in the book. If the reader requires personal assistance or advice, a competent professional should be consulted.

The author and publisher specifically disclaim any responsibility for any liability, loss, or risk, personal or otherwise, which is incurred as a consequence, directly or indirectly, of the use and application of any of the contents of this book.

Most Alpha books are available at special quantity discounts for bulk purchases for sales promotions, premiums, fund-raising, or educational use. Special books, or book excerpts, can also be created to fit specific needs.

For details, write: Special Markets, Alpha Books, 375 Hudson Street, New York, NY 10014.

Publisher: *Marie Butler-Knight*
Editorial Director: *Mike Sanders*
Managing Editor: *Billy Fields*
Executive Editor: *Randy Ladenheim-Gil*
Senior Development Editor: *Christy Wagner*

Production Editor: *Megan Douglass*
Copy Editor: *Jan Zoya*
Cover and Book Designer: *Becky Harmon*
Proofreader: *Mary Hunt*

Contents at a Glance

Contents

p. 45

p. 57

p. 83

p. 102

p. 107

p. 127

p. 137

p. 213

Introduction

At a recent sleepover, my daughter Kate pulled out yarn and crochet hooks and pronounced that she was going to teach her friend Delia to crochet. Delia resisted. She sat in a big red chair, arms folded over her little 8-year-old body, and watched. Kate first showed Delia how to chain and then wrapped her own little 8-year-old hands over Delia's and guided them to make a loop through a loop. Delia proclaimed, "I don't get this!" But she persisted, and soon she had several inches of chain. She took the yarn to bed (yes, I took it from her when she fell asleep!). The next day, she went home clutching skein, chain, and hook. She was, well, *hooked.*

I was 8 when I learned to crochet, and after making the endless afghan and the unwearable sweater and countless long, long scarves, I put it aside. I spent about a decade wallowing in quilting until the siren call of knitting beckoned. Knitting begat spinning begat weaving. And somehow in my huge fondness for all things fiber, I rediscovered crochet as yet another way to indulge that passion.

Crochet does things knitting cannot. Knitting is a fluid movement that produces a fluid fabric; if you want it to stand up, you have to felt it. Crocheting, on the other hand, does two very different things very well: it produces a solid, even sculptural, fabric that stands up on its own, and it produces a lacy fabric filled with air. Exploring the possibilities of the opposing forces is fascinating. And knitting combined with crochet can be truly amazing—just check out Chapter 12 to see how crochet can enhance knitting. I have attempted to lure knitters into the crochet fold, but they, like Delia, resist. Many of them, though, were nearly lured with the Sushi Roll-Up in Chapter 3 (made longer, of course, to hold their knitting needles).

If you're resisting, too, whether you knit or not—and you certainly do not have to know how to knit to crochet—dive into the projects in this book and see if there's something you want to make. Kate's personal favorites are the Cherry Bomb Backpack (Chapter 4), all the jewelry (Chapter 6) and, of course, her own art on the I Made This! Pillow (Chapter 10). I am partial to the Sleep Glasses (Chapter 11), but that might be the late-night crochet-a-thons talking.

See for your own self. Dig in. Wallow. Have fun. You'll soon be hooked, too.

How to Use This Book

Read the book like a child: flip through and look at the pictures. When you find a project you like, make it!

If you're a newbie, spend a bit of time with Chapter 1, learning about the tools of crochet. Fill up your crochet kit, pick out your yarns, and get to work. If you're a very beginner, you should stick with the yarn suggested—many of the projects are a happy marriage of design and fiber, and a third-party yarn might disrupt the union. Until you can feel the union of fiber and hook, it's tough to make yarn substitutions.

If you're a veteran, you can experiment with yarn from your stash, but for goodness sake, do a swatch! Read about it in Chapter 2, where you'll find a refresher course on stitches and techniques, as well as a list of crochet abbreviations. If you're a little rusty on these stitches, take a gander at the projects in Chapter 3. They're designed to help you limber up, with "sampler" projects that include several kinds of stitches.

Read through the instructions. And please, oh please, don't tell me you can't follow a pattern! Yes, you can! Chapter 2 will help.

And all the above is only **Part 1, "Getting Hooked."** In **Part 2, "At Home and Around Town,"** I give you projects to adorn your home and yourself—and maybe some worthy friends.

Then, in **Part 3, "Kids of All Ages,"** you explore the fun side of crochet with a mound of baby stuff, toys, and fun accessories. (After all, who doesn't need her own birthday hat?)

Part 4, "Beyond the Basics," is where you test your crochet talents by merging crochet with knitting and exploring new techniques, such as hyperbolic crochet and crocheting on a knitting loom.

And finally, at the end of the book you'll find a glossary and a list of further resources to explore the many techniques used in this book—take Tunisian crochet to the next level, for instance.

Extras

Along with all the info and instructions I've packed in the projects, you'll find some helpful hints in sidebars. Here's what to look for:

Check out these notes for crochet techniques and tips.

Be sure to read—and heed—these warnings meant to help keep you from getting tangled up.

What's yarn over mean? What's Tunisian crochet? Turn to these sidebars for explanations of crochet terms.

Make It Your Own

Ah, my favorite! Every project has suggestions for ways to make the project uniquely yours.

Acknowledgments

Many threads helped weave this book. These are the golden threads: Jacky Sach of BookEnds, LLC, who asked me if I knew anyone interested in writing a book on crochet projects. (Why, yes, I do!) Weta Ray Clark, who encouraged me to write a craft column for *The News & Observer* (Raleigh, NC). Without the column, Jacky never would have found me. Randy Ladenheim-Gil, the amazing Christy Wagner, and the rest of the team at Alpha Books, who were enormously patient and supportive. Debra Boyette, the most understanding boss in the world, who said my projects just might make her have to learn to crochet. The KnitWits, especially Julie Snee and Sarah Tacker, who provided key project-development advice and moral support. Ben Rice, my first-born, who provided technical assistance, great humor, and tremendous wisdom. Kate Rice, my second-born, who provided fabulous style sense and terrific patience. (Yes, we can go on a bike ride now!) Wimi, who made this book possible. Joe Miller, who makes all things possible.

Trademarks

All terms mentioned in this book that are known to be or are suspected of being trademarks or service marks have been appropriately capitalized. Alpha Books and Penguin Group (USA) Inc. cannot attest to the accuracy of this information. Use of a term in this book should not be regarded as affecting the validity of any trademark or service mark.

Getting Hooked

In This Part

All you need to get started crocheting is a hook and some yarn. But where to begin? So many enticing yarns beckon from the shelves—fuzzy, firm, bulky, thin. And the hooks—wood, bamboo, aluminum, plastic—what should you use?

This start-'em-up part helps you figure it all out. The stitch guide helps you explore different ways of looping the yarn together and to give you some practice with the various stitches, several "limber up" projects will have you stitching in no time.

Even if you're a veteran crocheter, you'll find some tips here—and some projects to draw on your stash!

Tools of the Trade

In This Chapter

The tool(s) of the crochet trade

Have you *seen* the yarn section?
What do I choose?!

I've got a notion …

Putting it all together

Unlike some hobbies you might have or think about picking up, crochet doesn't require a whole lot of tools or gadgets. All you really need are a hook, some yarn, and some know-how. And you're in the right place for all three.

In this chapter, I cover the tools you need to crochet—the previously mentioned hook as well as some other tools you might want to add to your crochet bag. I also help unravel all the yarns available to you (if you've seen your local yarn or craft store's yarn section, you know what I'm talking about) and offer some tips on how to pick the right *skein, ball,* or *hank* for your project. (Don't worry—I define all these terms in this chapter.)

As for the know-how … well, I've got that covered here, too.

Getting Hooked

If you've been crocheting for a while and think you know what a crochet hook is and does, don't skip over this section! You might just learn (or relearn) something.

The crochet hook, as you might guess, is the tool you use to loop a strand of yarn into crocheted *fabric*. The hook has five distinct parts: the point, the throat, the shaft, the thumb rest, and the handle.

? Fabric is what you're crocheting! Often we think of fabric as the woven kind you buy on a bolt and then cut into shapes. You can think of your crochet as fabric already "cut" to shape.

The *point* is the business end—it is the hook itself, along with the little pointy part that pokes under and around loops. With small hooks, the point is pointier; larger hooks have blunter points that don't catch on the bulkier yarns they're designed for.

The *throat* is the slender section between the point and the shaft. It's a little passage-way the yarn passes over on its way to the shaft.

The *shaft* is the portion of the hook that determines the size of the stitch, and it's this part of the hook referred to for sizing. The shaft's circumference matches the millimeter measurement.

The *thumb rest* is where you rest your thumb when crocheting. Often, the size of the hook is embossed on the thumb rest. Not all hooks have this part; some glide from shaft into handle. If your hook doesn't have a thumb rest, let your thumb rest in this general area anyway. It'll help guide your gauge so it's not too loose or too tight. (See Chapter 2 for more about gauge.)

The *handle* is the rest of the hook. It provides leverage, resting against your index finger or in your hand. Some han-dles are wide and/or cushioned for less hand strain. (See more about hook-holding methods later in this chapter.)

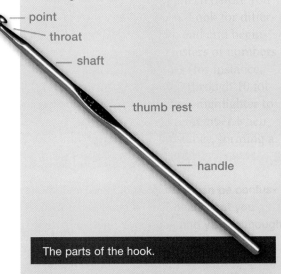

point
throat
shaft
thumb rest
handle

The parts of the hook.

What Size Hook Do I Need?

The international standard measure for crochet hooks is in millimeters (mm), much like knitting needles—and soon, thanks to the efforts of the Craft Yarn Council, all crochet hooks will be marked in millimeters. In the meantime, however, old packaging and old hooks may denote

Large, small, metal, plastic, wood—there's a world of crochet hooks you can choose from.

one of three or four different measuring systems—and some might not be marked at all! What's a crocheter to do?

The variety of crochet hook sizes—not to mention materials—can be overwhelming to the new crocheter.

First of all, know what you're measuring. The millimeters measure refers to the shaft of the crochet hook, *not* the handle. The point might be larger than the shaft, so if you have one of those nifty tools you can stick the hook through to find the size, it might not fit through the right hole. Look all over the hook to find a letter or number or something that indicates the size and then match it to the following chart. (The letters or numbers can vary. The millimeter number is more reliable.)

Midrange hooks (B through K) are made in aluminum, bamboo, acrylic, plastic, and wood. Larger hooks (L and up) are usually acrylic or plastic, although some are available in bamboo. Itty-bitty hooks (under 2.25 mm) are made of steel.

Crochet Hook Sizes

Steel Hooks		Aluminum, Bamboo, Wood, or Plastic Hooks	
Millimeter	U.S. Size	Millimeter	U.S. Size
0.75 mm	14	2.25 mm	B–1
0.85 mm	13	2.75 mm	C–2
1.00 mm	12	3.25 mm	D–3
1.10 mm	11	3.5 mm	E–4
1.30 mm	10	3.75 mm	F–5
1.40 mm	9	4 mm	G–6
1.50 mm	8	4.5 mm	7
1.65 mm	7	5 mm	H–8
1.80 mm	6	5.5 mm	I–9
1.90 mm	5	6 mm	J–10
2.00 mm	4	6.5 mm	K–10½
2.10 mm	3	8 mm	L–11
2.25 mm	2	9 mm	M
2.75 mm	1	10 mm	N
3.25 mm	0	11.5 mm	P
3.50 mm	00	15 mm	Q
		16 mm	Q
		19 mm	S

There's no clear rhyme or reason to crochet hook sizes. The mm sizes overlap for steel and aluminum hooks. Some hooks have letter and numbers; some just numbers. The elusive size 7 hook has no letter. There is no size A hook. Your best bet is to follow the mm guide. If the hook doesn't have a mm, use your gauge tool, but be sure to measure the shaft, not the handle.

So ... Which Hook Do I Use?

Depends on the yarn. Use tiny steel hooks for cotton thread and wire. Use midrange hooks for sport to worsted weight yarns. Save the big hooks for bulky yarns.

As far as what material hook to use: wood and bamboo warm nicely to your hand, but fuzzy yarns might not slide as well on them. Aluminum hooks are the classic workhorse of crochet, and they hold up well. I have a size J aluminum hook I've used since I was 8 years old. Having survived the larger hazard of being lost over the years, it has even retained much of its teal color.

You cannot have *too many* hooks. Sofas eat them; small boys use them to pry open cans; cats bat them under the furniture. If you can't find your K hook, buy a new one; the old one might show up eventually, but the hooks are cheap enough that you can have two.

Fancy-Dancy Hooks

Beyond the standard, run-of-the-mill crochet hooks, you might also see some fancy or just odd-looking hooks. What are these all about?

An *afghan hook* is used for—oddly enough—*afghan crochet,* or *Tunisian crochet.* It produces an even fabric that can look much like knitting. Its evenness also makes it ideal for embroidered embellishment, especially cross-stitch. You keep all the stitches live on the hook, like knitting, if you're familiar. You can crochet items only as long as the hook and then you have to join the strips together.

Tunisian or afghan crochet is a fusion of knit and crochet. Rather than working with a single live stitch, you pick up stitches across the row and then work them off. The result is a very sturdy fabric. (For more details, see Chapter 2.)

A *double-pointed hook* is also used for Tunisian crochet. It allows you to crochet with two colors, by sliding the work from one color at one end of the hook to a second color at the other end.

A *hairpin lace loom* is used to create strips of loops that can be joined together for an airy fabric.

The Sushi Roll-Up in Chapter 3 uses the afghan hook. If you're interested in exploring double crochet, check out the resources in Appendix B. The Olive Bowl in Chapter 13 draws on techniques similar to hairpin lace, but uses a different tool; look for emerging hairpin lace patterns in very recent crochet magazines.

Some crochet hooks don't even look like normal crochet hooks. Left to right, these are a double hook, an afghan hook, and a hairpin lace loom.

How to Hold a Hook

You'll find your own way to hold a hook as you get more crochet proficient. You might find when you get started that there are as many methods of holding a crochet hook are there are crocheters. But here are two basic methods: the pencil grip and the knife grip. Try them both and see what works for you!

The pencil grip provides good control over the crochet work, as it's easier to insert the hook and maintain gauge. This is the method I use most. The disadvantage is that if you go on a crochet spree, this method eventually wears on your wrist.

You can hold the crochet hook like a pencil …

The knife grip is easier on your wrist and allows for quick crochet work, once you get used to it. Lily Chin, the world's fastest crocheter, uses this grip. I use this method when I'm working with a very heavy yarn or want to keep a loose gauge.

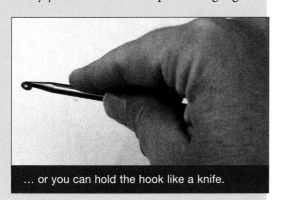

… or you can hold the hook like a knife.

Tensioning the Yarn

While you're holding the yarn and the hook and making your stitches, you also have to pay attention to your yarn tension. It's important to keep the yarn taut while you're working with it. It's kind of like kite string—if you don't keep some pull on the string, the kite will dip and swoop as it likes.

To maintain the tautness, or tension, use your left hand to guide the yarn. First loop the yarn around your pinky (the back-up tension, like the spool holding the kite string), and run the yarn behind your index finger (like your hand guiding the kite string). Let the yarn run through your fingers evenly. It shouldn't be so tight that your pinky starts to turn purple, but it shouldn't just fly through either. With a little practice, you'll find the right tension to make it work.

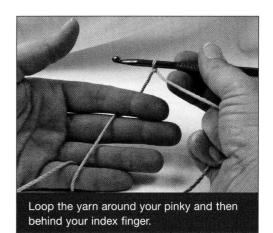

Loop the yarn around your pinky and then behind your index finger.

Yarn and Other Fibers

The wealth of yarns and crochetable fibers available is the main reason crochet is moving so forcefully into the twenty-first century. In this book, you'll see I use a variety of fibers, from the humble acrylic of our fore-crocheters to sumptuous wool blends and sleek cottons to downright fancy, make-your-teeth-hurt-expensive silk and lurex and fairy-spun blends. The best way to ensure that you'll finish a project is to find a yarn you love and then figure out what you'll make from it—that's the way most of these projects were born.

It can get overwhelming to stand in front of all the available skeins or balls of fiber at your *local yarn shop* (*LYS*). It helps to know what you're looking at, so in the following sections, I give you an overview of how to make the yarn work for you.

? LYS is your local yarn store. If you don't know of a specialty yarn store near you (check your phone book or online), this could be the yarn section of a local craft and hobby store.

Natural Fibers

Wool, available in a plethora of colors and weights, is fabulously crochet-able. Cotton is a classic crochet fiber, offering its services for countless potholders and doilies. The new softer cottons, especially the organics, make lovely baby goods as well as sweaters *pour vous*.

What could you make with this medley of cottons with a touch of bling?

Or these wool yarns in vibrant hues?

This is better-than-doily cotton.

Mohair is a lovely fluffy fiber, sometimes blended with wool to create a sturdy fabric with just a bit of fluff. Cashmere, made from the belly fluff of a goat, is super-soft and painfully expensive. Alpaca, sometimes called the poor fiber artist's cashmere, is pretty soft, too. Yak and opossum are exotic fibers that are pretty nice if you can get them.

Unnatural Fibers

You've seen them—the garish greens and outrageous oranges twisted into rippled fabrics on the backs of couches across America circa the 1960s and 1970s. If that image makes you want to skip this section—wait! Synthetic fibers are so much nicer than they used to be.

All sorts of flitty fibers—with bitty bobbles and lush lashes and faux fur—offer enormous design possibilities. Because it's so hard to see the stitches—and, therefore, where to put your hook—in that fluffy stuff, you might want to save these fancy things for trim. Ribbon yarns and railroad yarns can be tricky to work with, but they do create lovely fabric.

Synthetic fibers are scrumptious nowadays.

Use ribbon and railroad yarns for a fun change of pace.

Unconventional Fibers

Wire, twine, surveyor's tape, torn-up garbage bags—these are the materials of both thrift and art. Look around you. What other seemingly everyday things can you find to crochet into a work of art? Don't be afraid to try new things and experiment with your materials.

Yarn Packaging

Yarn is packaged and sold in three forms: skeins, balls, and hanks. A *skein* is probably what you're most familiar with—that oblong, machine-wound bundle you or someone you know has probably used as a makeshift football. Skeins usually weigh about 8 ounces and are very easy to use once you find the end in the center.

A *ball* works like a skein: you pull the yarn end from the center to start working. If it's mohair or something equally fuzzy, work from the outside—the fiber can get all tangly if you pull from the inside. Balls are usually smaller, about 4 ounces or less.

A *hank* (or sometimes called a skein to make it confusing) is a large loop of yarn.

Most often, it's been hand-spun or hand-dyed and hasn't been wound into a ball yet, hence the loop. You have to wind it in a ball before you use it, either by hand, using a chair back, or bribing a friend with strong arms to hold the skein. Or you can use a ball winder and swift. Many yarn shops wind hanks for you, sometimes for a small fee. Whatever you do, don't try to crochet the yarn directly from a hank or you'll end up with a mess.

Whatever the form the yarn comes in, the label provides a wealth of information in addition to the yarn name. Take a look:

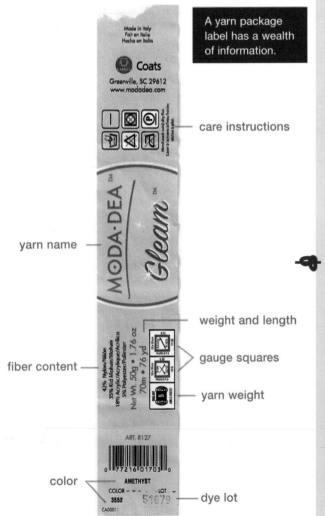

A yarn package label has a wealth of information.

- care instructions
- yarn name
- fiber content
- weight and length
- gauge squares
- yarn weight
- color
- dye lot

Fiber content shows the makeup of the yarn. It might be a single fiber, or it might be a blend. If the latter, it will show percentages of each kind of fiber.

Color is listed as both name and number. Some do not have a name, only a number. If you're using more than one skein or ball of the same color, be sure the *dye lot* number is the same on all the balls. Some hand-dyed balls don't have dye lots.

Weight and length are listed in grams and/or ounces and meters and/or yards. This is the weight of the bundle of yarn you hold in your hand. *Yarn weight*, on the other hand, is indicated by the little yarn ball icon with a number in it, a device created by the Craft Yarn Council. This icon shows the heft of the strand of yarn itself. The yarn is numbered from 1 to 6, super fine to super bulky. (See the table at the end of this chapter.)

You're going to hear a lot about gauge in the following chapters. On the yarn label, the *gauge square* lists the suggested crochet hook and knitting needle size to obtain the gauge given. Note that your gauge might be different (see Chapter 2).

Frequently, in this knitter-centric world, the label will *not* indicate suggested crochet hook size. So you'll have to do a little work. Find the recommended knitting needle size, then convert the millimeter to crochet size hook.

The care instruction symbols indicate whether to wash by hand or machine, at what temperature, drying instructions, and ironing instructions. The X means *don't do this.*

Notions

All you really need to crochet is yarn and a hook. But a few other things will make your crocheting life easier.

Get yourself a good *gauge tool*. This handy tool helps you convert the mm (millimeter) of the knitting needle to the mm of the crochet hook (labels are often knitting-biased and don't include a crochet hook size). Match the mm to the knitting needle size and then look on the other side of the hole in the gauge tool to find the corresponding letter size of the crochet hook. Then go up a size (the conversion from knitting to crochet is not usually equal). Do your gauge swatch, of course, to see if that hook works with your yarn and your tension—this tool has a little window for checking your gauge.

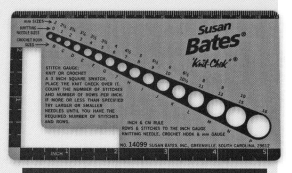

A gauge tool is indispensable.

Stitch markers help you count rows and to mark stitches where you begin and end your work. Be sure to pick up the split markers—the closed markers are for sliding on knitting needles. You can use fancy, beaded markers, too—but, again, get the kind that clip on, not the sliders.

Stitch markers—you'll quickly learn to appreciate these little things.

Scissors, of course. It's so much nicer than using your teeth or getting yarn burns on your hands from trying to snap the yarn apart. If you work with wire, you'll also need *wire cutters* so you don't trash your scissors.

A cut above: scissors and wire cutters.

A *measuring tape* helps you see how far you've come and how far you have to go.

Need a 4×4-inch square? Get out your measuring tape.

You'll need *tapestry needles* and *sewing pins* for weaving in ends and sewing pieces together. The pins hold the pieces together while you sew with the needle.

Handy and necessary—pins and needles.

Finally, keep a *notebook* on hand. If you're following a pattern, it will help you keep track of your progress. It also helps you keep track of your projects: write down the project name, the pattern source, the yarn used, when you started, when you finished, and, if you give it away, the recipient. Note any changes you made to the pattern. Staple the yarn label to the page so you have both the dye lot number and care instructions (if you give the item away, write down the care instructions on a little card for the giftee). Poke a couple holes in the page and tie a little bow of the yarn into it. You can even paste in inspiration pieces and draft patterns of your own.

Use a notebook to track your projects and ideas.

Getting It Together

Beautiful crochet is born of marrying your hook and yarn in a happy union. The Craft Yarn Council has developed a Standard Yarn Weight System (www.yarnstandards.com) for helping crocheters find the best tool for the yarn. Look for the little yarn ball weight measurement on the label. If you don't see one, determine the weight on your own, based on the description (fingering, worsted, bulky, etc.). Then test a hook in the recommended range. The following table provides a quick cheat sheet.

Overall, trust your own intuition and design sense. If you don't want a standard-weight fabric, adjust your hook size. If you want a denser fabric for a rug or toy, for instance, use a smaller hook. If you want an airy fabric for a shawl, use a larger hook. It's your game, after all. Play!

Yarn, Gauge Ranges, and Recommended Hook Sizes

Yarn weight	Super Fine 1	Fine 2	Light 3	Medium 4	Bulky 5	Super Bulky 6
Type of yarns in category	Sock, Fingering, Baby	Sport, Baby	DK, Light Worsted	Worsted, Afghan, Aran	Chunky, Craft, Rug	Bulky, Roving
Crochet gauge ranges in single crochet to 4 inches	21 to 32 sts	16 to 20 sts	12 to 17 sts	11 to 14 sts	8 to 11 sts	5 to 9 sts
Recommended hook (metric)	2.25 to 3.5mm	3.5 to 4.5mm	4.5 to 5.5mm	5.5 to 6.5mm	6.5 to 9mm	9mm and larger
Recommended hook (U.S.)	B–1 to E–4	E–4 to 7	7 to I–9	I–9 to K–10½	K–10½ to M–13	M–13 and larger

Refresher Course

In This Chapter

Whether you're new to crocheting or have been taking hook to yarn for decades, it's always good to have a little refresher. (When's the last time you made a double triple crochet? Could you do one now without looking it up?) And maybe I can show you a few things in this chapter even you experienced crocheters didn't know yet. In the upcoming projects, you'll combine these basics in different ways. And if you're a newbie with the crochet hook, you may see that it's not all that hard to learn!

Crochet Abbreviations

If you've flipped ahead to some of the patterns, or looked at some crochet patterns in your LYS or online, you probably noticed the abbreviations used in crochet patterns. *Ch 3, 1 dc in each sc across, end 1 dc in tch—* say what? Why not just write it out? Here's why: because *Chain 3, double crochet in each single crochet across the row, ending with 1 double crochet stitch in turning chain—*that's three times longer! Plus, it's kind of cool having a crochet shorthand—like having a secret language. The following table provides a quick abbreviations cheat sheet to keep you in the loop until you can talk the talk yourself.

Crochet Abbreviations

ch	chain
cl	cluster
dc	double crochet
dec	decrease
dtr	double triple crochet
hdc	half-double crochet
inc	increase
r	row or round
rep	repeat
sc	single crochet
sk	skip
sl st	slip stitch
tch	turning chain
tog	together
tr	triple crochet
ttr	triple triple crochet
yo	yarn over
()	indicate a pattern that is repeated a given number of times
*	indicates the starting and ending place of a pattern repeat

Don't worry about memorizing all these right now. I'll talk about them throughout the chapter, and you can bookmark this page so you can flip back to it easily when you need to.

Introducing the Stitches

Crochet stitches are like building blocks, ranging from small (single crochet) to tall (double crochet) to very tall (triple crochet) to crazy tall (double triple crochet and triple triple crochet). They "grow" with the addition of loops on the crochet before you insert the hook into the row below.

More on these and other stitches coming up. First, though, you need a base chain.

Chain (ch)

To make a *chain,* start with a *slip knot:* loop the yarn so it makes an X (you can wrap it around your fingers to do this). Stick the hook through the loop, hook the yarn (not the tail), and pull the knot tight.

Make an X and pull the loop through.

Pull the loop through and tighten to make a slip knot.

To make a chain, wrap the yarn over the hook and pull the yarn through the loop onto the hook—but don't pull it too tight! That's 1 stitch. Continue until the chain is as long as called for (in inches or stitches).

The chain is the base foundation of nearly every other crochet stitch.

Loosen up! If your starting edge is curved, your starting chain is probably too tight. Remember, you have to get the hook into those little loops to make your starting row.

Most patterns call for a few more chains than you need to make the stitches in the first row. The extra chains are *turning*

chains, and they bring the work up the height of the stitch you're working. Think of the turning chains as the stepladder up to the next row.

If you're working single crochet, you need 2 chains (1 for the turn and 1 for the height of the stitch). For double crochet, you need 3; 4 for triple crochet; and so on. So for a start row of 10 single crochets, you need 12 chains; for 10 double crochets, you need 13 chains. You then begin work in the third chain for single crochet, in the fourth chain for double crochet, and so on.

Some patterns call for variations on the number of chains other than what I list here. That's likely because of the stitch pattern used. Just follow the directions.

Where Do I Put the Hook?

Good question. There are a few places to insert the hook in the chain. Each gives a different effect.

Inserting the hook under the V gives the cleanest edge to the work. You stick the hook under the V formed by the top of the chain and then complete the stitch as directed.

Insert the hook under the V.

You could also insert the hook under the top loop and the "hump." This is the way I always inserted my hook, before I knew there were other ways to do it. It gives a pretty clean edge and is easier than inserting the hook under the V—a method that requires a bit of manipulation until you get used to it.

Insert the hook under the top loop and the "hump."

Next, you could insert the hook under the top loop only. This is the easiest method of all, but it leaves a very loopy, jagged sort of edge, good if you're looking for that effect. It's also where to put the hook when you are making a "sliding loop," where you want to be able to tighten the yarn, say at the center of a circle (see "Making a Circle" later in this chapter).

Insert the hook under the top loop only.

Finally, you can insert the hook under the "hump." This method leaves a very neat-looking edge with a tidy row of V's along the edge. It does requires some concentration, though. It's also the magic method knitters use for a provisional cast-on, because the chain can be "unzipped" easily, leaving live loops for the knitter to knit. The other methods entangle the yarn, so that you can't "unzip" it without using scissors.

Insert the hook under the hump only.

Slip Stitch (sl st)

The slip stitch is a flat stitch, sort of the landing before the staircase. To make it, insert the hook into the top of the stitch below, yarn over, and pull through the loop on the hook.

To make the slip stitch, pull a single loop through the loop on the hook.

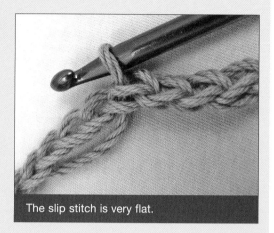

The slip stitch is very flat.

Single Crochet (sc)

The single crochet is the smallest of the stitches. To make it, insert your hook through the top of the stitch below (or into the starting chain), *yarn over,* and pull through both loops on the hook.

? Yarn over means you wrap the yarn over the hook from back to front. This gives you another loop to work with. Use your left index finger to hold the yarn taut while you finish the stitch.

Making the single crochet.

The finished single crochet.

The Second Row

When you begin working your second row of stitches, work under both loops of the stitch in the row below unless the pattern calls for something different.

Working under 2 loops on the second row.

Double Crochet (dc)

The double crochet is a tall stitch. To make it, yarn over and insert your hook through the top loop of the stitch below. Yarn over and pull through first 2 loops on hook and then yarn over again and pull through 2 last loops.

To double crochet, first wrap the yarn over your hook.

Then insert your hook into the stitch and wrap the yarn over.

Next, pull the loop through first 2 loops on your hook.

Finally, yarn over and pull through the second 2 loops on the hook.

Half-Double Crochet (hdc)

The half-double crochet is a handy stitch. Less dense than the single crochet and less leggy than the double crochet, it provides coverage without bulk. To make it, yarn over and insert hook through the top loop of the stitch below, as if to make a double crochet. Then yarn over and pull through all 3 loops on hook.

The half-double crochet looks like the beginning of a double crochet.

But instead of pulling through just 2 loops like a double crochet, you pull through all 3 loops on your hook.

Combining stitches to create fabric is fun stuff. For instance, single crochet and half-double crochet combine to create a lovely texture. Try it out with His Scarf in Chapter 8.

Triple Crochet (tr)

Triple crochet shows up often enough, usually to make the tallest part of a flower (see Chapter 3) or create a lacy look. To make it: yarn over 2 times and insert your hook through the top loop of the stitch below. Yarn over and pull through the first 2 loops on the hook. Yarn over and pull through next 2 loops. Yarn over and pull through 2 last loops.

For triple crochet, yarn over with 4 loops on your hook.

Pull loop through 2 loops.

And then 2 more loops …

Finally, pull through the final 2 loops. See the 3 (triple) ridges in the stitch?

Double Triple Crochet (dtr)

These super-tall stitches are used most often in threadwork to create lacy doilies. I used double triple crochet in the Big Doily (see Chapter 7), but sparingly. To make the double triple, work as for the triple, but wrap the yarn 3 times and then (yarn over, pull through 2 loops) 4 times.

A double triple. Note the 4 ridges.

? Parentheses in a pattern indicate a step that is to be repeated. The number of repeats is given right after the closing parenthesis.

Triple Triple Crochet (ttr)

The triple triple, the tallest of the stitches, works up pretty much like the double triple, except for the triple triple, wrap the yarn 4 times and (yarn over, pull through 2 loops) 5 times.

A 5-ridge triple triple.

There you have it—all the stitches you'll ever need! You can combine these stitches in so many different ways to form patterns, as you'll see in the projects in this book.

Now, time for one more special stitch before we get into some techniques for working with the basic crochet stitches.

All the stitches, small (left) to tall (right): slip stitch, single crochet, double crochet, triple crochet, double triple crochet, triple triple crochet, and quadruple triple!

Tunisian Stitch

The Tunisian (or afghan) stitch is sort of a fusion of knitting and crochet that produces a very sturdy, woven-looking fabric. It's usually worked on a long afghan hook (see Chapter 1), but for work that's not very wide, you can use a regular hook.

Tunisian (or afghan) stitch.

To do it, begin with a starting chain. Then pick up loops in each chain across, leaving each loop on the hook. When you reach the end, do not turn (the right side always faces you in this stitch; others might flip back and forth depending on what direction you're going).

With the loops picked up across, get ready to return.

To do the return row, yarn over and pull through 2 loops on the hook. Repeat, pulling through 2 loops each time, until you reach the end.

Pull a loop through 2 loops.

On the second row (the forward), insert your hook under the vertical bar of the second stitch in the row below and pick up a loop in each vertical bar across. Repeat the return row.

Pick up a loop in each vertical bar.

Repeat these 2 rows—forward and return—for the pattern. To bind off, begin on right side of row, with 1 loop on your hook. Slip stitch across by inserting your hook in second vertical bar, pulling up the loop, and pulling it through the loop on the hook. Repeat across.

Bind off with slip stitches from right to left.

A Few More Techniques

With all the basic stitches under your belt, now let's look at a few more techniques that will take your crocheting to the next level. Have fun playing and experimenting with these techniques.

Increasing (inc) and Decreasing (dec)

Squares are fine, but sometimes you want to make your work smaller or larger, as in shaping a sweater or making a toy. That's when knowing how to *increase* and *decrease* comes in handy. You can do the increasing or decreasing subtly or dramatically, depending on what you're making.

To increase subtly, simply work 2 stitches into 1. Note that if you do several increases in a single row, the row will curve a bit. If you do several increases close together, you'll create a bubble on the fabric. To try this method in its extreme, take a stab at the Hyperbole Earrings in Chapter 13.

A subtle increase.

To decrease subtly, work 2 stitches together. For example, to do this with double crochet, insert your hook in the first stitch of decrease and work half of a double crochet (yarn over and pull through first 2 loops on hook). Insert your hook in the second stitch and work half of a double crochet. Yarn over and pull through all the loops on your hook. As with increasing, if you do several decreases in a single row, the row will curve a bit.

A subtle decrease.

To do dramatic shape-shifting, you use the lowliest of stitches: the slip stitch and the chain stitch. To increase, chain 1 fewer than the number of stitches you want to add, plus the number of chains to equal a stitch. So to increase 5 double crochet, chain 7: 4 chains + 3 chains that counts as 1 double crochet = 5 double crochet. Turn. Double crochet in the fourth chain from the hook and then in the next 3 chains. Continue to double crochet across the row.

To dramatically decrease, slip stitch across the top of the stitches to the point where you want to begin stitching again. Make enough chains to bring you up to the height of the stitch you're using (1 or 2 for single crochet; 2 or 3 for double crochet).

A dramatic increase.

A dramatic decrease.

Going in Circles

Now that you know how to make increases and decreases, let's really work some shapes, starting with circles. You can form circles by crocheting *in the round* with regular increases. If you attach each round—joining the final stitch to the first stitch with a slip stitch—you have an evenly spaced circle. If you work the rounds without joining, you create a spiral.

A circle, worked by joining the last stitch to the first stitch with a slip stitch and then "climbing" to the next row with chains.

A spiral, worked by continuing to crochet the next round without joining the first and last stitches of each round.

You can start a circle in one of two ways. One is to join chains into a loop. This leaves a small hole in the center.

Join chains with a slip stitch to form the center circle.

To minimize the center hole, make a loop, leaving a tail. Work stitches into the loop and then pull the tail to tighten the center. This is a sliding loop. Cool, huh?

Work stitches into the first loop and then tug the tail to tighten the circle.

You can make circles with any size stitch, but because of the height difference, each stitch requires a different number of starting stitches and increases per round to create a flat circle.

For single crochet:

R1: In starting chain, make 6 sc.

R2: 2 sc in each sc (12 sc).

R3: (1 sc in sc, 2 sc in next sc) around (18 sc).

R4: (1 sc in each of next 2 sc, 2 sc in next dc) around (24 sc).

R1, R2, R3, etc.—what do these mean? The R stands for "round" when making a circle and "row" when making any other shape. You'll see a lot of these in the patterns!

Continue in this pattern, evenly increasing 6 stitches each round by increasing the number of single crochets between increases by 1 for each round.

For double crochet:

R1: In starting chain, chain 3 (counts as 1 dc), make 11 dc.

R2: 2 dc in each dc (24 dc).

R3: (1 dc in dc, 2 dc in next dc) around (36 sc).

R4: (1 dc in each of next 2 dc, 2 dc in next dc) around (48 dc).

Continue in this pattern, evenly increasing 12 stitches each round by increasing the number of double crochets between increases by 1 for each round.

If your circle is buckling as you work, it's due to either a tight gauge or too-frequent increases. If changing to a larger hook doesn't help the problem, work fewer increases.

For triple crochet:

R1: In starting chain, chain 4 (counts as 1 tr), make 17 tr.

R2: 2 tr in each tr (36 tr).

R3: (1 tr in tr, 2 tr in next tr) around (54 tr).

R4: (1 tr in each of next 2 tr, 2 tr in next tr) around (72 tr).

Continue in this pattern, evenly increasing 18 stitches each round by increasing the number of triple crochets between increases by 1 for each round.

The more frequent the increases in a circle, the rounder it will appear. So the double-crochet circle, with 12 increases per round, is rounder in appearance than the single-crochet circle, which has 6 increases per round and tends to look more like a hexagon than a circle.

After you make a base circle, if you continue working in the round without increasing, you'll make a tube of sorts. You can try this with the Bowled Over pattern in Chapter 5. A tube with sharper increases makes a cone, as with the Birthday Hat in Chapter 11. A circle with increasingly tall stitches makes the Nautilus Coaster in Chapter 5.

Noodle around and see what you can create with these practice circles. Call them coasters. Squeeze one in the middle, add beads, and make a flower pin. Turn some into pockets on a bag, sweater, or pillow. Sew some on to a ribbon to make a garland. Or hang the beribboned circles in a doorway. Sew a couple together to make a tote or a PDA cozy. If one turns out a bit wonky, keep it and turn it into something else.

Squares

Squares worked in the round are a lot like circles, except you add the increases at just four points to make the corners. An advantage of working a square in the round is that you don't have to know ahead of time how big your square needs to be—you stop when it's big enough.

A square worked in the round.

To make a square in the round, make a chain loop.

R1: Ch 1, then make 12 sc in ring. Join to first sc with a sl st.

R2: Ch 1, 1 sc in first sc, *3 sc in next sc, 1 sc each of next 2 sc, rep from * around, ending with 1 sc in final sc. Join with sl st to first sc.

R3: Ch 1, 1 sc in each of first 2 sc, *3 sc in next sc, 1 sc each of next 4 sc, rep from * around, ending with 1 sc in final 2 sc. Join with sl st to first sc.

Continue around, increasing evenly 4 times on each round by working 3 sc in each corner stitch.

If you want a little decorative hole in the corner, instead of working 3 scs, work (1 sc, ch 1, 1 sc) in the corner. On each round, work increases in ch-1 space.

Perhaps the most famous of the crochet squares—and my editor's favorite thing to crochet—are granny squares, made by working a series of shell stitches in the round, with extra shells at the corners to make it square. Traditionally, granny squares were a way to use up leftover yarn, so each round was in a different color. Like chocolate-chip cookies, there are as many granny square variations as there are bakers. To try my recipe, check out the Granny Squared Bag in Chapter 4.

A granny square.

And now that you know how to single crochet, you can, of course, make a square by crocheting back and forth in rows until you have a square. You can also work a square on the diagonal, as with the Point-Counterpoint Blanket in Chapter 9.

Shells, Popcorn, Bobbles, and More

You can work shells, popcorn, clusters, and bobbles in any size stitch, but they're most often done in double crochet. The 4 stitches are really just variations on the same stitch but produce different looks.

To make a *shell,* work double crochets in the same stitch. The number of stitches depends on the pattern. This is ultimately a horizontal stitch. Shells are good for making a fancy edging, and they make a luxurious fabric, as with the Maximal Mini Skirt and the Dogwood Wrap (both in Chapter 7).

A shell with 5 double crochets.

A *popcorn* is similar to a shell, but after working the double crochets in the same stitch, you remove the hook, reinsert it in the first stitch of the group, and hook the loop from the last stitch into the first stitch. The result is a "popped" stitch that's vertical rather than horizontal.

A popcorn with 5 double crochets.

Remove your hook, insert it into the first stitch of popcorn, grab the loop from the last stitch, and pull it through.

The *bobble* is similar to the popcorn, except instead of working the full stitch, you work only the first part of each double crochet, keeping the final loop on the hook. After doing the final double crochet, you yarn over and pull through all the loops on the hook. Usually worked on the wrong side of the fabric, the bobble "pops," but not quite as much as the popcorn.

A bobble with 5 double crochets.

A cluster with 5 double crochets.

Pull the final loop through all the loops on your hook.

Pull the final loop through all the loops on your hook.

The *cluster* (cl) is similar to the bobble, except you work the partial double crochets in separate stitches rather than the same stitch (though a cluster is sometimes worked in a chain loop). After doing the final double crochet, yarn over and pull through all the loops on the hook. This stitch is very rounded and more horizontal than the bobble. Worked in tandem with a shell stitch on the following row, the cluster forms a Catherine's Wheel (see the Cherry Bomb Backpack in Chapter 2).

Crocheting in the Back Loop

Crocheting in the back loop creates a ridge. If this is done on both sides of the fabric, it creates a stretchy rib stitch. Done once on one side, it creates an edge.

To crochet in the back loop, instead of working the stitch into both loops of a stitch, insert your hook just in the back loop. Then make the stitch as usual.

Crocheting in the back loop.

Joining Yarn and Changing Colors

To join yarn to a piece of fabric, insert your hook at the designated spot and draw up a loop. Yarn over and pull through the loop. (Be sure you're not working with the short tail of the yarn!)

Joining new yarn with a slip stitch.

Changing Colors Without Cutting Yarn

To join new yarn as a color change in the middle of a piece, join it as the final loop of the last stitch you worked. Pick up loop of new yarn, and draw it through the last 2 loops of the other yarn.

Join a new color in the final loop of the row.

Pull the loop through.

If you're working just a row or two in a new color, you can carry the old yarn up the side the rejoin without cutting it.

Carry the old yarn up the side and rejoin it in the final loop.

Ending Off

The final stitch secures the fabric so all the work you put in doesn't come unraveled—literally. To secure, cut a tail at least 6 inches long and pull it through the last loop, creating a teeny knot at the end.

Pull the yarn end through the final loop.

Weaving in the Ends

Weaving in the ends—nobody likes to talk about this pesky task. Some folks leave them dangling and call it art. But the piece is not really done until the ends are woven in. You'll develop your own favorite way to tuck them in, but here's a way I do it.

Thread the yarn onto a tapestry needle. Working on the back of your fabric, weave the needle through a few loops and draw through. Go backward and reinsert the needle, then go forward again through a few stitches. When you're satisfied that the tail is secured, cut yarn close to final stitch.

Weaving in the ends.

Doing a little back step for extra security.

Go long! A frequent rookie error is frugally cutting the tail much too short. This is bad (just ask my editor, who can't use her first afghan anymore because the ends are unraveling!). Cut the tail at least 6 inches long so you have enough to thread on a needle and properly weave back in.

Seaming

Sometimes you can join your work by starting with a new color where you left off with the first color, as described in the preceding section. But sometimes you have two separate pieces of fabric you need to join. You can't really take your crocheted fabric to your sewing machine and sew everything together, but you can still sew your pieces together by *seaming*.

As with other fabrics, when you join two pieces, you want to be sure you align the two right sides with the ends (or points designated by pattern) meeting. Pin the fabric at intervals to keep it even.

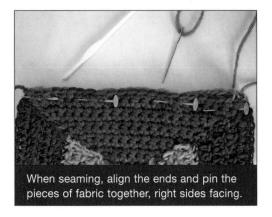
When seaming, align the ends and pin the pieces of fabric together, right sides facing.

You have a few choices when it comes to the method you use to join the seams. Keep reading to learn more about these stitches.

Whipstitch Seam

This is the quick-and-dirty, yet pretty sturdy, seam. It's usually worked on the wrong side, unless you want the whip-stitching to show as a decoration.

To whipstitch, thread a tapestry needle with matching yarn. With right sides together, sew, pushing the needle and thread in one side and out the other of the top/outside loops, creating a diagonal line along the edges.

The whipstitch seam.

Woven Seam

A bit subtler than the whipstitch, the woven stitch is also worked on the wrong side. With a tapestry needle, weave the yarn back and forth through the right-sides-together fabric, pushing the needle first from one side and then the other, moving down a bit each time.

The woven seam.

Slip Stitch Seam

Worked from the wrong side, the slip stitch provides a really sturdy seam where you need it, for example, on a tote bag or toy. To do it, work slip stitches evenly along the seams, working through both layers of fabric.

The slip stitch seam.

Worked from the right side, the slip stitch seam can make a nifty ridge.

Single Crochet Seam

This is a seriously sturdy seam, good for areas that need a seriously sturdy seam, like on market bags. Or treat it like a decorative element and work it from the front. This can create a nice frame—for instance, the black borders that often join colorful granny squares for a blanket. To do it, single crochet along the seam edge, working through all layers.

The single crochet decorative seam.

Chain Loops Seam

This lovely stitch—which isn't a seam so much as a join—is often used to join flower motifs for sweaters. For this join, do not pin the fabric right sides together. Instead, lay them side by side, about as far apart as you want them in the finished piece. Single crochet in one side, make enough chains to reach the other side, and single crochet in the other side. Continue zigzagging to the end of the seam.

The chain loops seam.

Final Touches

That's a lot of "refresher course"—but we're not done yet! You need to know a few more final touches and techniques before I send you off into the project chapters.

Blocking

Blocking your work evens out stitches and smoothes out the fabric. This is especially important if you're working with pieces that need to fit together neatly—for instance, squares for a blanket. It also makes just about any garment look neater.

To block, pin the work to the desired shape, mist lightly with water, and let sit until dry. (I pin it to a craft board, which has the inches marked on it.) Or use a steam iron to mist the fabric—hold the iron about an inch over the fabric and give a short burst. Then pin to shape and let dry. (See Chapter 5 for more on blocking.)

Don't iron the fabric! Ironing mashes the stitches and, in the worst case, melts, burns, or disfigures the yarn. If you need to get out some wrinkles, hold the iron about an inch over the fabric and give it a burst or two of steam.

Felting

Felting is a technique of shrinking your project—on purpose. Felting softens fabric and compacts the stitches to make a sturdier finished piece. Felting is used just occasionally with crochet, because crochet produces a sturdy fabric anyway—much sturdier than knitting, which employs felting more often.

To felt, you need to expose the fabric to three elements: water, soap, and agitation—specifically warm water, a bit of soap, and lots of agitation. A spin or two in the washing machine usually does it. In the process, the crocheted fabric shrinks about 20 percent—about half as much as knitting shrinks with the same process. Try out felting with the Granny Squared Bag in Chapter 4.

Getting Gauge

Finally, what's all the fuss about gauge? What is gauge even? Gauge is what happens when yarn, hook, and crocheter come together.

Crochet and knitting patterns call for a recommended hook size but often also carry the caveat "or size needed to obtain gauge." Why can't they tell you that already? Because every crocheter crochets at a different tension—and even the same crocheter can have different energy moving into the work at different times. That's why it's important to do a gauge swatch. If your gauge is off by half a stitch in your swatch, then your sweater will be off by a couple inches.

Because gauge is a reflection of your energy, it's also a measurement of your mood. If you're crabby, you'll probably crochet tighter. You might want to keep a "moody project" around that can take the edge off when you need it.

Before you start a project, you need to make a swatch using the yarn and the hook size you'll use for the project. Make the swatch in the called-for stitch at least 4×4 inches square. This allows you to get a true measurement of how many stitches you're making. If, for instance, you get $2\frac{1}{4}$ stitches in 1 inch, you would miss the partial stitch in a 1×1-inch swatch. But in a 4-inch swatch, it would add up to a full stitch.

Once you have your swatch, measure it. Compare what you've got—how many stitches per inch—to the gauge called for in the pattern. If you have more stitches, switch to a smaller hook. If you have fewer stitches, try a larger hook. If you're designing your own work, use the hook that produces a stitch that looks and feels right to you.

Same yarn, different hooks.

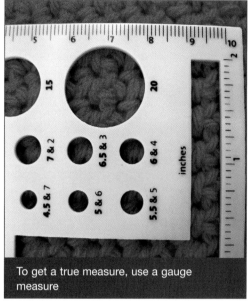

To get a true measure, use a gauge measure

Same yarn, same hooks, different crocheters.

If you work up several swatches with different hooks, tie on a little tag noting the yarn, hook size, and gauge. It takes just a second and you'll be grateful once you decide on the right gauge.

Okay, having said all that about gauge, here's a thought: if you're working on a blanket or cat toy, don't sweat gauge that much. But do be sure you're in the ball park—so your cat doesn't end up with a blanket you intended for yourself.

Caring for Your Crochet

Okay, you've spent some time making this *objet d'art*—so use it already! But when you clean it, be sure to follow the directions on the yarn's label. And unless you're felting something, don't put any of it in the washer. Washers chew things up and spit them out smaller, fuzzier, and generally unsuitable for anything but kitty blankets. Instead, wash garments by hand in mild soap and swoosh gently; don't scrub them around. Lay flat to dry out of direct sunlight.

You *can* put the items you made with Sugar and Spice cotton—the Mess Blocker Washcloth and Love That Bib in Chapter 9, for instance—in the washer. They'll shrink a little, but they're supposed to. They get happier with age.

How to Read a Pattern

You're nearly there! I just want to cover one more thing: how to read a crochet pattern. After all, you can't turn that ball of yarn into a crocheted thing of beauty if you don't understand the directions.

With each pattern, I've indicated the *skill level:*

/ = Pretty easy.

// = You might want to have a bit of experience under your crochet belt before trying this.

/// = You definitely need to be alert for this one!

These are just suggestions. Don't let a three-hook project keep you from tackling a project if you really love it. And some don't indicate the level of stitch difficulty so much as the level of patience required (for instance, the Hyperbolic Earrings in Chapter 13 are a three-hook project, not because of the simple single crochet, but because they're done with thread and a teeny hook).

Gauge: Indicates the gauge used for that project, or how many rows and stitches in the stitch indicated equal 4 inches. Test it out and adjust your hook size until you match the gauge given.

To make sense of the symbols, see the list of abbreviations in the beginning of this chapter. Here are a few more symbols to look for:

Asterisks (*) indicate a part of the pattern that's to be repeated. This is usually for a row pattern, and will say "rep from *." So you go back to the asterisk and repeat the pattern.

Parentheses ( ) do the same thing as asterisks, but they usually indicate a smaller pattern. For instance, it may say (ch 1, sc) 5 times, which means that you chain 1, make a single crochet 5 times, and then continue on with the rest of the pattern instructions.

Read over the whole pattern before you pick up your hook or yarn. Look for differences in the pattern at the end and beginning of a row. Look for clusters of numbers that indicate repeated rows (for instance, R5–R10 means that rows 5 through 10 follow the same pattern). Use a highlighter to mark places you want to remember when you do the pattern (for instance, forming a buttonhole).

Sometimes reading a pattern can be confusing. You can't see in your head what you need to do with your hook and yarn (although I've included *lots* of pictures to help you along!). So after you finishing scratching your head, go ahead and plunge in. If you're working with a fussy or pricey yarn, test the pattern with cheaper yarn first. But use the good stuff for your swatch so you get a true measurement.

So now you're ready! Take off!

Limber Up

In This Chapter

Fashionable Hair Scrunchies
to keep your hair out of your eyes
(so you can see to crochet!)

A fun Bean Counter Bag
to hold … beans?

Brighten your day with a Rosy Posy

Mark your page with a
Bunch of Bookmarks

Hungry? Try the
Sushi Crochet Hook Roll-Up

This chapter is designed to warm up your fingers for the projects ahead. Nearly every skill you need throughout the book is included in these little projects. You begin with a simple chain stitch Hair Scrunchie and then move on to the Bean Counter Bag with its basic single crochet. The Sushi Crochet Hook Roll-Up has 6 pattern stitches, including a lacy stretch fabric and Tunisian crochet.

In this chapter, you'll find a couple specific-use bags, but most you can use for just about anything. So carry on!

These Hair Scrunchies give you some limbering up on chain stitch as well as introduce you to working with novelty yarns. And you'll be able to pull your hair back with something a little classier than a newspaper rubber band! No hair to pull back? These make great presents.

Try your hand at these fun Hair Scrunchies.

Fashionable
Hair Scrunchies

Using two ponytail holders reduces the chances of the holder breaking. Plus, if one breaks, the other will still hold.

Scrunchie 1

Close-up of scrunchie 1.

1 R1: Holding 2 ponytail holders together, join yarn around holders with sl st. Sc around holder, completely covering ring (45 to 50 sts).

Join your yarn around the holders with a slip stitch.

Skill level:
1

Yarn:
Scrunchie 1:
Berroco Cotton Twist Variegated (70% mercerized cotton, 30% rayon, 50 g, 85 yd.), 1 skein Pinata Mix 8447

Scrunchie 2:
Red Heart (100% acrylic, 8 oz.), a bit of Black 0312 (A); Trendsetter Sorbet (65% viscose, 20% polyester, 15% metal), 1 ball Livie 1032 (B)

Crochet hook:
H (5mm)

Notions:
Ponytail holders

Finished size:
4 inches in diameter

Gauge:
Varies

Work in the back loop only on the first round.

To hide the tail, hold it against the ponytail holder and crochet over it.

R2: Do not turn. *Working in back loop only,* *ch 5, sc in back loop, rep from * around.

R3: Do not turn. *Working in front loop only,* *ch 5, sc in front loop, rep from * around.

Cut yarn. Weave in ends.

Scrunchie 2

Close-up of scrunchie 2.

R1: Holding 2 ponytail holders together, join A around holders with sl st. Sc around holder, completely covering ring (45 to 50 sts).

R2: Do not turn. Join B. *Working in back loop only,* *ch 5, sc in back loop, rep from * around.

R3: Do not turn. *Working in front loop only,* *ch 5, sc in front loop, rep from * around.

Cut yarn. Weave in ends.

Make It Your Own

For these scrunchies, use whatever yarn tickles your fancy—or matches your wardrobe. Or add some bling to your outfit for a just a few bucks by stringing on some beads and securing them randomly with the chain stitch.

Bean Counter Bag

Looking like a remnant from Woodstock, this little colorful bag adds some bling and carries your things—a few coins or charms or whatever you don't want to fall out the hole in your pocket. It's worked in single crochet in a spiral pattern, with a few double crochets to hold the drawstring.

This fun necklace bag holds your goodies.

Skill level:
///

Yarn:
Berroco Cotton Twist Variegated (70% mercerized cotton, 30% rayon, 50 g, 85 yd.), 1 skein Fiesta Mix 8452

Crochet hook:
F (3.75mm)

Notions:
Tapestry needle
Stitch marker

Finished size:
3¼ inches in diameter

Gauge:
Single crochet 6 stitches and 5 rows equals 1 inch

Use a stitch marker to mark the beginning of each round.

With wrong sides facing, single crochet the edges together, leaving 10 stitches unworked.

When working a spiral, don't join each round. To keep track of rounds, put a stitch marker in the first stitch of each round, moving it each time you start a new round.

Here's the circle formula: each round, you increase the same number of times as the stitches in the first row. So if you start with 6 stitches, the next round has 12, the next 18, the next 24, and so on. To make the shape rounder, start with more stitches.

Sides (make 2):

Ch 4. Join with sl st to form ring.

R1: In ring, work 6 sc. Do not join.

R2: Work 2 sc in each sc (12 sc).

R3: *Sc in 1 sc, 2 sc in next sc. Rep from * around (18 sc).

R4: *Sc in each of 2 sc, 2 sc in next sc. Rep from * around (24 sc).

R5: *Sc in each of 3 sc, 2 sc in next sc. Rep from * around (30 sc).

R6: *Sc in each of 4 sc, 2 sc in next sc. Rep from * around (36 sc).

R7: *Sc in each of 5 sc, 2 sc in next sc. Rep from * around (42 sc).

R8: *Sc in each of 6 sc, 2 sc in next sc. Rep from * around (48 sc).

Break off yarn for side 1. Make side 2. When side 2 is done, do not break yarn.

R9 (joining sides): Holding wrong side together, sc sides together along edges. Leave 10 sts unworked.

R10 (top opening): On one side only, sc in 10 sts. Then, without cutting yarn, sc in 10 sts along other side. Join to first sc with sl st.

R11: Dc in each st around opening on both sides. Join with sl st to first dc.

R12: Sc in each st around opening on both sides. Join with sl st to first sc.

Cut yarn. Weave in ends.

3 Make a chain 30 inches long or to desired length to wear as a necklace. Weave tie between dcs, using hook to pull it through.

Weave the tie through the top of the bag.

Make It Your Own

Make a bigger bag by using thicker yarn and a bigger crochet hook. No need to change the number of stitches—the different gauge does all the work!

A crocheted flower can add a nice touch to just about anything. You can alter the size and appearance of the flower simply by using different thicknesses of yarns. Here, the same colors are used, but you could easily substitute different colors. In fact, these flowers take so little yarn to make, you can have a whole rainbow of colors.

One flower, three ways.

Rosy Posy

The petals of these flowers are made with the shell stitch, which you learned in Chapter 2.

All the flowers follow the same pattern. Let's go!
With A, ch 8. Join with sl st.

R1: Ch 1. Work 15 sc into ring. Join with sl st into first sc. Do not turn. (Flowers are worked from the front side only.)

To avoid having to weave in the ends later, hold the ends down and crochet over them as you go.

R2: Ch 5, sk first 3 sc, *sl st into next sc, ch 5, sk 2 sc. Rep from * to end. Sl st into sl st from previous r. Five chain-5 spaces made. Break off A.

1 **R3:** Join B with sl st in any ch-5 loop. In loop, work 1 sc, 1 hdc, 2 dc, 1 tr, 2 dc, 1 hdc, 1 sc. Rep in each ch-5 loop around. Join with sl st to beginning of first petal.

1

Join the new color with a slip stitch into the chain-5 loop.

Skill level:
1 1 1

Yarn:
Flower 1: Coats & Clark Royale Fashion Crochet Thread 3 (100% mercerized cotton, 150 yd.), 1 ball each Tangerine 0325 (A) and Warm Rose 0775 (B)
Flower 2: Lily Sugar 'n Cream (100% cotton, 2.5 oz., 120 yd.), 1 ball each Hot Orange 01628 (A) and Hot Pink 01740 (B)
Flower 3: Lamb's Pride Bulky (85% wool, 15% mohair, 4 oz., 125 yd.), 1 skein each Lemon Drop M-155 (A) and Rosado Rose M-183 (B)

Crochet hook:
Flower 1: E (3.5mm)
Flower 2: G (4.25mm)
Flower 3: K (6.5mm)

Notions:
Tapestry needle

Finished size:
Flower 1: 2¾ inches in diameter
Flower 2: 4¼ inches in diameter
Flower 3: 5¾ inches in diameter

Gauge:
Varies

Chain stitch behind the petals.

A closer look at the petal construction.

2 **R4:** Working behind petals, *ch 8, join with sl st between base of next 2 petals, and rep from * around.

3 **R5:** In ch-8 loop, work 1 sc, 1 hdc, 3 dc, 1 tr, 3 dc, 1 hdc, 1 sc. Join with sl st to first sc of first petal.

Cut yarn. Weave in any ends.

Make It Your Own

Make a garden of blooms! Glue or sew a pin to the back and wear your flowers on a sweater or hat or use to pin a wrap. Or loop a flower over a button for a quick pick-you-up.

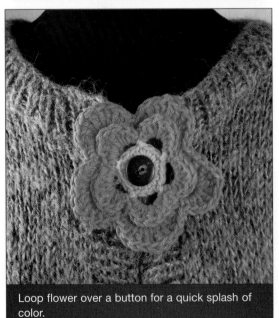

Loop flower over a button for a quick splash of color.

A Bunch of Bookmarks

These bookmarks keep your place in a book. Or think of them as lots of tiny little presents already done—just pop one on the top of the next book you give away. Meanwhile, you can see how yarn behaves when it's crocheted. For instance, putting a lot of stitches in 1 stitch over and over makes the fabric curl up. And adding a few stitches at the edge makes it flare out. I love using Red Heart yarn for these little projects; it's durable, colorful, and very forgiving if you have to tear it out and plant a new bloom.

A bunch of blooming bookmarks.

Skill level:
///

Yarn:
Red Heart Super Saver Multicolor (100% acrylic, 5 oz., 278 yd.), small amounts Bikini 0929 (A), Candy Print 0786 (B), Banana Berry 0994 (C), Sunshine Print 9798 (D), and Bright Yellow 0324 (E)

Crochet hook:
H (5mm)

Notions:
Tapestry needle

Finished size:
Squiggle: 16 inches long
Rose: 14 inches long; bloom is 2 inches in diameter
Calla: 14 inches long; bloom is 1¾ inches long

Gauge:
Varies

Squiggle

Squiggle bookmark.

With A, ch 17.

R1: In fourth ch from hook, work 3 dc (first 2 ch count as 1 dc); work 4 dc into each of the next 12 ch. Sl st into last ch. Ch 60. Turn.

R2: (You're now working at the end opposite the big squiggle.) In fourth ch from hook, work 3 dc. Work 4 dc into each of the next 6 ch. Join with sl st to sixth ch. Cut yarn, leaving 8-inch tail.

Thread tail on needle and weave through chains worked. Pull tight, forming a saucer-like shape. Tie a knot, and weave end in.

Rose

Rose bookmark.

Bloom:

With B, ch 22.

R1: Sc in third ch from hook, (ch 1, sc) in each ch across. Turn.

R2: Ch 2, *5 sc in next ch-1 space, sl st in next ch-1 space. Rep from * across. Cut yarn, leaving a long tail.

1 Coil up bloom, tight in the center. Use the tail to sew the coil in place.

Coil up the bloom, and sew it in place.

Stem and leaf:

Join C at base of flower. Ch 62. Turn.

R1: In second ch from hook, work 1 sc. Working 1 st in each ch, work 1 hdc, 3 dc, 1 hdc, 1 sc. Sl st in next ch. Turn.

2 **R2:** Working down ch on side opposite you just worked, work 1 st in each ch: 1 sc, 1 hdc, 3 dc, 1 hdc, 1 sc.

Cut yarn. Weave in ends.

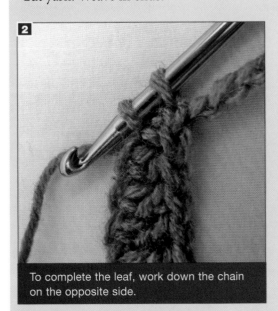

To complete the leaf, work down the chain on the opposite side.

Calla

Calla bookmark.

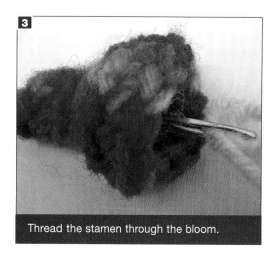

3

Thread the stamen through the bloom.

Bloom:

With D, ch 2.

R1: In second ch from hook, work 6 sc. Do not turn. Do not join.

R2–3: *Working in back loop only* (here and throughout) sc in each sc. Do not turn.

R4: Work 2 sc in each sc.

R5: Work 1 sc in each sc. Join with sl st to first sc on this round.

Cut yarn. Weave in end.

The end of the stamen is a cluster. Turn back to Chapter 2 if you need to take another look.

Stamen:

With E, ch 8. Work sc cluster: insert hook in second ch from hook and pull up loop. Leaving loop on hook, insert hook in 3rd ch from hook and pull up loop. Yo and pull through all 3 loops on hook. Cut yarn, leaving a 6-inch tail. Pull tail through final loop, and use a tapestry needle to weave it through to the end of the stamen.

 Thread E ends on needle and pull through flower.

Stem:

Join C, and ch 50. Cut yarn and pull through last ch.

Weave in ends.

Make It Your Own

With some fat yarn, you can turn these bookmarks into scarves! These super-skinny scarves would be more fashion statement than chill-blockers.

This project is a fun way to tote around your crochet tools—when you roll it up, it looks like a vegetarian sushi roll! And it's a true sushi sampler: it includes 6 stitches, including Tunisian crochet. The stretchy yarn used for the lacy hook holder lets you slide in a variety of sizes of hooks so you won't lose them. And although I know you're not the showing-off type, you'll be able to showcase your skills every time you take out your hooks at a yarn meeting.

Sushi Crochet Hook Roll-Up—unwrapped and showing off its contents.

Sushi Crochet Hook Roll-Up— all wrapped up.

Sushi Crochet Hook Roll-Up

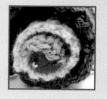

A close-up of single crochet in the back loop in carrot and cucumber and single crochet through both loops in ginger.

Sushi, anyone? Here's how you prepare the ingredients: With A, ch 32.

R1: Sc in second ch from hook and across (30 sc). Ch 1 tch.

R2–3: Sc in back loop only, ch 1 tch. Join B in tch of R3

R4–6: With B, Sc in back loop only. Join C in tch of R6.

R7–10: With C, Sc in both loops, ch 1 tch. Join C in tch of R10.

1 **R11–34:** Work rice stitch across: * sk 1 st; 2 sc in next st, rep from *, ch 1 tch. Rep row. On row 35, join E in tch.

Rice stitch close-up.

Skill level:
111

Yarn:
Kristin Nicholas Julia (50% wool, 25% kid mohair, 25% alpaca, 50 g, 93 yd.), 1 ball each Carrot 2250 (A), Spring Green 585 (B), Harvest Gold 2163 (C), Natural 0010 (D), and Velvet Moss 6086 (E); Cascade Fixation (98.3% cotton, 1.7% elastic, 50 g, 100 yd.), 1 ball Persimmon 4447 (F)

Crochet hook:
F (3.75mm),
G (4.25mm)

Notions:
Tapestry needle
Needle and thread
for sewing

Finished size:
15½ inches long by
7 inches tall

Gauge:
Double crochet 16 stitches and 10 rows equals 4 inches

Nori stitch close-up.

It's easy to lose count with rice stitch! Be sure to mark off rows as you do them, using an old-fashioned pencil and notepad.

2 **R35–55:** Work nori stitch: ch 2 *5 dc, 5 sc, rep from *. Turn. Ch 2.

Break off yarn. Weave in ends.

Tie:

With E, ch 5.

R1: Insert hook in second ch from hook and pull up a loop. Leaving loop on hook, pull up a loop in each of next 3 ch.

R2: Work off loops: *yo, pull first 2 loops, from left to right. Rep from * until 1 loop remains.

Repeat rows 1 and 2 until piece is 22 inches long, ending with row 2.

Tie close-up.

The tie is worked with Tunisian stitch. See Chapter 2 for a refresher.

Cut yarn and weave in ends.

3 Fold tie in half, and sew at the midpoint to the center edge of the roll.

Hook holder:

With yarn F and hook F, ch 19.

R1: In fourth ch from hook, work (2 dc, 1 ch, 1 sc), *sk 3 ch, in next ch (2 dc, 1 ch, 1 sc), rep from * to last 3 ch, sk 2 ch, 1 dc in last ch. Turn.

R2: Ch 2. *In ch-1 space, work (2 dc, 1 ch, 1 sc), sk (2 dc, 1, sc), repeat from *, ending with 1 dc in tch.

Repeat row 2 until piece is $15\frac{1}{4}$ inches long, or until it extends along the length of the roll without stretching.

Center hook holder on case and sew on with needle and thread, which will secure the hook holder firmly.

Lace close-up. This fabric holds your crochet hooks

At Home and Around Town

In This Part

Done with toilet-tissue covers? Yeah, so am I. Ditto the jackets that look like blankets and frumpy scarves. In Part 2, you'll find cool accessories for your home and for yourself.

Try the retro wrap skirt or maybe a delicate beaded crochet necklace. Need to whip up some presents in a hurry? Check out the scarves or the quick cozy blanket. (The latter is really an over-size doily, but you don't have to tell anyone!) You might want to start off with one of the bags—to carry your works in progress. Pick it up, put it on, and wear it with style!

In the Bag

In This Chapter

Take note! with the
Grab-and-Go Notebook Bag

Enjoy the view with the
Blue Ridge Panorama Tote

Make a statement with the
Cherry Bomb Backpack

Put a new twist on the granny with the
Granny Squared

There's no such thing as *too many bags,* and that's especially true if you're a craftperson—you can have a separate bag for every project! A bag is a fabulous way to play with color. It doesn't have to match what you're wearing—in fact, the more outstanding it is, the better! Let a bag brighten your day by making it in your favorite colors—or by trying out an experimental combination. The Cherry Bomb Backpack in particular has a fun design for playing with color.

A nice thing about bags is that gauge doesn't matter so much. You can play with pattern and texture and not worry too much about how big or small it is. In the meantime, you'll learn a lot about how a pattern shapes fiber and how some stitches can be quite sturdy.

In this chapter, you'll find a couple of specific-use bags, but most you can use for just about anything. So carry on!

I have a swell little notebook I use to jot down ideas. I made a bag for it so I could carry it with me everywhere. The bag has three ways to tote it: a grab-and-go slit handle, a long strap for slinging it around my body (if the strap stretches over time, tie an overhand knot in the top), and a carabiner (who says they're just for mountain climbing?) for clipping it to my pack or belt loop. The stretchy Fixation yarn keeps the notebook snug and lets me slip a pen inside, too.

You'll never be without a place to jot down your thoughts with this Grab-and-Go Notebook Bag.

Grab-and-Go Notebook Bag

You crochet in the round in this project. For a refresher if you forgot from Chapter 2: to start crochet in the round, start with the V of your hook facing you (the hump is to the back). Stick the hook under the top 2 loops to make a single crochet. At the end, work 2 single crochets in the end chain, turn the chain, and work single crochets back across in the remaining loop.

Ch 26.

1 **2** **R1:** Sc in front loop of second ch from hook, then sc in front loop of next 24 sts. 2 sc in last st. Sc in back loop of sts. Sc in last st. Join to first st with sl st (52 sc). Place marker at beginning of round.

Single crochet across 2 loops.

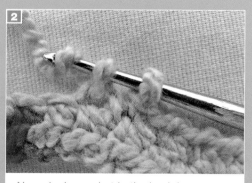

Now single crochet in the back loops.

Skill level:
///

Yarn:
Cascade Fixation
(98.3% cotton, 1.7% elastic, 50 g, 100 yd.), 1 ball 9478

Crochet hook:
Size 6 steel (1.8mm)

Notions:
Carabiner
Tapestry needle

Finished size:
4¼ inches wide by 6½ inches long

Gauge:
24 stitches and 30 rows of single crochet equals 4 inches by 4 inches

Skip 14 chains and then join the chain with a single crochet.

Crochet across top of the chain to make the handle.

Join the long handle with a single crochet on the opposite side.

R2–43: Sc in both loops of every st, ending on the same side that round began. The piece will measure about 5¾ inches.

For the first few rounds, the piece will look floppy and funky. Stick with it! As you crochet more rounds, it will shape up.

R44: (shaping the handle) Sc in first 6 sc. Ch 14; sk next 14 sts. Sc in next 12 sts. Ch 14; sk 14 sts. Sc in final 6 sts.

R45: Sc in first 6 sts; sc across 14 ch, across 12 sts, across 14 sts, to end.

R46–50: Sc in all stitches. End on same side as beginning. Do not cut yarn.

Strap:

Ch 230 (or as long you like). Join with sc to opposite side of bag. Turn. Sc in front loop only of second ch from hook. Sc to end, in front loop only. Turn. Sc in back loop to end.

Cut yarn. Weave in ends. Hook carabiner to handle.

Make It Yours

Make this bag whatever size you need. Make one to tote your PDA or iPod, or a small crochet project, or just enough stuff to go out on the town: sunglasses, money, keys. Just crochet enough chains to go across the front and one side of the PDA, iPod, or sunglasses and then add just a stitch or two. (Remember that Fixation will stretch just a bit.)

Blue Ridge Panorama Tote

Inspired by the sun setting behind the Blue Ridge Mountains in North Carolina, this bag is just right to hold a crochet project, along with a cell phone, wallet, and perhaps a wish or two.

The wrapped cotton of Mission Falls 1824 Cotton makes a solid, sturdy bag, especially when used doubled. Using a sampler of stitches, the bag is a perfect project for expanding your crochet repertoire.

You can almost see the mountains and the dusk sky in this Blue Ridge Panorama Tote, can't you?

Skill level:
11

Yarn:
Mission Falls 1824 Cotton (100% cotton, 50 g, 84 yd.), 1 ball each Moss 304 (A), Fennel 301 (B), Wintergreen 302 (C), Indigo 404 (D), Chicory 401 (E), Sky C403 (F), Coral 201 (G), and Cosmos 203 (I); 2 balls Lilac 406 (H)

Crochet hook:
K (6.5mm)

Notions:
Tapestry needle

Finished size:
16 inches wide by 10 inches tall

Gauge:
Double crochet 10 stitches and 5 rows equals 4 inches

Notes:
Use yarn doubled throughout

This project uses double yarn throughout. To use doubled yarn without buying 2 balls of yarn, pull a strand from outside the ball and a strand from the inside of ball.

(Make 2 pieces; front and back are the same.)
With A, ch 41.

R1: Sc in second ch from hook and in every ch across (using both loops) (40 sts). Turn.

R2: Ch 2. Dc in every sc across (40 sts). Turn.

R3: Join B. Ch 1, *sc 5, work 1 *long st* (insert hook 2 rows below, yo and pull loop up even with row being worked, yo and pull through both loops on hook to complete sc), rep from * to last 4 sc; sc in last 4 sc (40 sts). Turn.

To make a long stitch (also called spike stitch), insert the hook a row or more below the row you're working, yarn over, draw loop up even with the row, and complete stitch. The stitches can be different lengths depending on where you insert the hook.

R4: Ch 2. Dc in every st across (40 sts). Turn.

R5: Join C. Ch 1. Sc 3, *1 long st 2 rows down, sc 5, rep from * to last 6 sc. Sc in last 6 sc (40 sts). Turn.

R6: Dc, increasing in tenth, twentieth, and thirtieth sts by working 2 dc in single st (43 sts). Turn.

R7: Join D. Ch 1. 4 sc, *sk 3 sc, 7-dc shell in next sc, sk 3 sc, 7 sc; rep from * to last 4 sc; end with 4 sc (3 shells). Turn.

When making a shell, slip a stitch marker into the next stitch. This keeps you from losing that stitch as the shell base stitch expands.

R8: Ch 1. Sc across (43 sts). Turn.

R9: Join E. Ch 2, 3-dc shell in first sc, *sk 3 sc, 7 sc, sk 3 sc, 7-dc shell in next sc; rep from * across; end 4- dc shell in last sc (2 shells, 2 half shells). Turn.

R10: Ch 1. Sc across (43 sts). Turn.

R11: Join F. Ch 1, 4 sc, *sk 3 sc, 7-dc shell in next sc, sk 3 sc, 7 sc; repeat from *, ending with 4 sc (3 shells).

R12: Ch 1. Sc across (43 sts). Turn.

R13: Join G. Sc across (43 sts). Turn.

R14: (Begin long wave stitch.) Ch 3, 2 tr, *2 dc, 2 hdc, 3 sc, 2 hdcs, 2, dcs, 3 trs; rep from * across, ending with 2 tr (2 full waves, 2 half waves). Turn.

R15: Ch 1, sc across (43 sts). Turn.

R16: Join H. Ch 1, 2 sc, *2 hdc, 2 dc, 3 tr, 2 dc, 2 hdc, 3 sc; rep from * across ending with 2 sc (3 full waves). Turn.

R17: Ch. 1, sc across (43 sts). Turn.

R18: Join I. Ch 3, 2 tr, *2 dc, 2 hdc, 3 sc, 2 hdc, 2, dc, 3 tr; rep from * across, ending with 2 tr (2 full waves, 2 half waves). Turn.

R19: (Shape handle.) Ch 1, sc 15, ch 13, sk 13, sc 15. (It might help to place stitch markers after sts 15 and 26.)

R20: Join H. Sc across all sc and ch (43 sts). Turn.

R21: Ch 2. Dc across (43 sts).

Cut yarn. Weave in ends.

2. Using the whipstitch method and holding right sides together, sew side and bottom seams. With bag still inside out, fold bottom corner in the opposite direction. About 1 inch from point, sew a line perpendicular to seam line, using a running stitch.

Make a lining if you want, and sew into place.

This is how your handle should look now.

The bottom of this bag is nice and boxy—to hold more stuff without looking too stuffed!

The Cherry Bomb Backpack an easy bag to wear, keeping your essentials nearby but safe and out of your way. It's good for a day trip at a festival, and because it's made with washable acrylic, you don't have to worry about getting it dirty. But really the most fun thing about this bag is the cool pattern stitch, called Catherine's Wheel. Like magic, when you do 7 half-stitches in a row and pull the yarn through all 8 loops, it swoops up into a semi-circle. A 7-stitch shell on the return trip finishes out the "wheel." It makes you feel very clever, indeed!

My daughter laid claim to this Cherry Bomb Backpack before it was even done.

Cherry Bomb Backpack

Front:

With A, ch 52. Turn.

R1: Sc in second ch from hook and in next ch *sk 3 ch, 7 dc in next st, sk 3 ch, 3 sc; rep from *, ending with 2 sc. Turn.

R2: Attach color B (do not cut A). Ch 2. Work 4-dc cluster over (sc, sc, dc, dc), * ch 3, sc in next 3 dc, ch 3, work 7-dc cluster over (dc, dc, sc, sc, sc, dc, dc); rep from *, ending with ch 3, 4-dc cluster over (dc, dc, sc, sc). Turn.

 Need a refresher on shells and clusters? Check out Chapter 2.

R3: Ch. 2. 4-dc shell in top of cluster, *sk ch 3, 3 sc, sk ch 3, 7-dc shell in top of cluster; rep from *, ending with 4-dc shell in top of cluster. Turn.

R4: Draw A, still joined, up side and join with a chain. Sc in next 2 dc, *ch 3, 7-dc cluster over (dc, dc, sc, sc, sc, dc, dc), ch 3, 3 sc; rep from * across, ending with 2 sc.

Repeat rows 1 through 4 six more times, ending with row 4. The piece should measure about 12½ inches. Break off yarn.

Skill level:
/ / /

Yarn:
Reynolds Signature (80% acrylic, 20% wool, 100 g, 220 yd.), Chocolate 030 (A), Rose 84 (B), Turquoise 026 (C)

Crochet hook:
G

Notions:
2 (½-inch) beads
Tapestry needle

Finished size:
11 inches wide by 13½ inches tall

Gauge:
Catherine's Wheel motif (rows 1 through 4): over 10 stitches equals 1¾ inches; half-double crochet: 13 stitches and 9 rows equals 4 inches

You can make the back of the Cherry Bomb Backpack in a complementary or contrasting color.

Back:

With C, ch 41. (No, that's not a typo. The back starts with 10 fewer stitches. The pattern stitch on the front "eats up" the width.)

R1: Hdc in second ch from hook and across (40 sts). Turn.

R2–36: Ch 1, hdc across (40 sts). Turn.

The piece should measure about 12½ inches, same as front.

Assembly:

With right sides facing you, attach A at upper-left corner of front. Work sc down the left side, across the bottom, and up the right side of front.

When working in a pattern, the edges usually end up looking pretty ragged. Even them up by working a row of single crochet down the side. This makes it easier to sew the pieces together.

With right sides of front and back together, chain stitch to join the side and bottom seams.

Weave in ends. Turn bag right side out.

Top edging:

R1: Join A at back side seam. Sc in each st across. For front: sc in 2 sc, *2 sc in ch 3 space, 1 sc in shell, 2 sc in ch-3, sc 3; rep from * across. Join with sl st to first sc.

R2: Ch 3 (counts as 1 dc), dc in second st from hook. *Ch 1, sk 1 st, dc in next st; rep from * around, join to top ch-3.

R3: Hdc in dc, hdc in ch-1; rep from * around, join to top of ch-2 (80 hdc). Cut yarn.

Handles:

Make 2 twisted cords: cut 2 (8-yard) pieces of C. Fold one piece in half and then in half again. Attach loop to a door handle or loop it over a friend's finger (ask first!). Twist, twist, twist in the same direction until you have 4 strands twisted together. Tie a knot in both ends (not too tight—you'll be taking them out in a little bit). Repeat with other cord.

1. Thread 1 cord through eyelets at top, starting and ending at the same side.

Use your crochet hook to pull the knotted end from the back to the front at the
2. bottom corner of the bag. Pull the end through a bead and tie a knot.

Repeat with second cord, starting and ending at the opposite side.

Make It Yours

Color, color, color: the design on the front of this pack is well suited to any two colors: turquoise and brown, purple and green, black and anything. The back can match or contrast. And if you have your own designer beads, use them!

Thread the cord through the eyelets, beginning and ending on the same side.

Push the cord from the back to the front at the bottom corner and then push through the bead and tie a knot.

The granny square is probably the most crocheted pattern through-out history. And with all those granny squares around, some cro-cheters are probably sick of seeing them! That's where this project comes in. Although it uses 4 granny squares, they're arranged in such a way and then felted. You'll hardly recognize them!

Granny Squared—this isn't your grandmother's granny square project!

Granny Squared

One of the original color-change yarns, Kureyon moves smoothly from color to color, with often a "surprise" color in the middle. When you're gawking at the display at your LYS, remember to stick to the wool yarns for this project so you can felt it. The granny square has enough air in the design that when the bag is felted it's still flexible—and those holes close up so you don't lose your goodies. You might still want to add a lining, so you have a place to put your phone and mints. This version is done in earthy colors, but use whatever makes you happy. The edging and handles take a small amount of wool; use whatever you have on hand that works with the colors.

 When a project is to be felted, as this one is, be sure to use wool yarn only, as only wool will felt. If you substitute any yarn, be sure it's wool. Do not use superwash wool; it is designed *not* to felt.

Granny squares (make 4, 2 each of colors A and B):
With A or B, ch 6. Join with sl st to form ring.
R1: Ch 3 (counts as 1 dc); make 2 dc in ring, *ch 3, 3 dc. Rep from * 2 more times (4 shells), ch 3. Join with sl st to top of first ch-3. Do not turn.

 For a smooth look, do not turn when doing rounds. Instead, with right side facing you, "scoot" the yarn over to the next chain-3 space by doing a couple of slip stitches.

R2: Sl st in top of second st from hook; sl st in ch-3; ch 3 (counts as 1 dc); 2 dc, ch 3, 3 dc, ch 1; *in next ch-3, 3 dc, ch 3, 3 dc, ch 1; rep from * 2 more times (4 corner sets). Join with sl st to top of first ch-3. Do not turn.
R3: Sl st in top of second ch from hook; sl st in ch-3; ch 3 (counts as 1 dc); 2 dc, ch 3, 3 dc, ch 1; *in ch-1, 3 dc, ch 1; in next ch-3, 3 dc, ch 3, 3 dc, ch 1; rep from * 2 more times. In final ch-1, 3 dc, ch 1; join with sl st to top of first ch-3. Do not turn.

Skill level:
11

Yarn:
Noro Kureyon (100% wool, 50 g, 100 m), 2 balls each colors 92 (A) and 78 (B); CC Lite Lopi (100% wool, 50 g, 109 yd.), Eggplant 417 (C); Lamb's Pride Worsted (85% wool, 15% mohair), Kiwi 191 (D)

Crochet hook:
J (6mm)

Notions:
1 (1¾-inch) wood bead
Tapestry needle

Finished size:
Prefelted, each square is 11½ inches; felted, squares are about 10 inches; bag is 13 inches by 13 inches on the diagonal

Gauge:
Finished size: single granny square: 11½ inches, before felting; 4 squares sewn together: 25 inches
After felting: Each square is 10 inches. Bag is about 12 inches deep, 12 inches wide.

Sew 2 squares together along 1 side.

R4: Sl st in top of second ch from hook; sl st in ch-3; ch 3 (counts as 1 dc); 2 dc, ch 3, 3 dc, ch 1; *in next 2 ch-1, 3 dc, ch 1; in next ch-3, 3 dc, ch 3, 3 dc, ch 1; rep from * 2 more times. In each of last 2 ch-1, 3 dc, ch 1; join with sl st to top of first ch-3. Do not turn.

R5: Sl st in top of second ch from hook; sl st in ch-3; ch 3 (counts as 1 dc); 2 dc, ch 3, 3 dc, ch 1; *in next 3 ch-1, 3 dc, ch 1; in next ch-3, 3 dc, ch 3, 3 dc, ch 1; rep from * 2 more times. In each of last 3 ch-1, 3 dc, ch 1; join with sl st to top of first ch-3. Do not turn.

R6: Sl st in top of second ch from hook; sl st in ch-3; ch 3 (counts as 1 dc); 2 dc, ch 3, 3 dc, ch 1; *in next 4 ch-1, 3 dc, ch 1; in next ch-3, 3 dc, ch 3, 3 dc, ch 1; rep from * 2 more times. In each of last 4 ch-1, 3 dc, ch 1; join with sl st to top of first ch-3. Do not turn.

R7: Sl st in top of second ch from hook; sl st in ch-3; ch 3 (counts as 1 dc); 2 dc, ch 3, 3 dc, ch 1; *in next 5 ch-1, 3 dc, ch 1; in next ch-3, 3 dc, ch 3, 3 dc, ch 1; rep from * 2 more times. In each of last 5 ch-1, 3 dc, ch 1; join with sl st to top of first ch-3. Do not turn.

R8: Sl st in top of second ch from hook; sl st in ch-3; ch 3 (counts as 1 dc); 2 dc, ch 3, 3 dc, ch 1; *in next 6 ch-1, 3 dc, ch 1; in next ch-3, 3 dc, ch 3, 3 dc, ch 1; rep from * 2 more times. In each of last 6 ch-1, 3 dc, ch 1; join with sl st to top of first ch-3. Do not turn.

R9: Ch 3 (counts as 1 dc); 2 dc in each of next 2 dc *in ch-3, 5 dc, dc in each dc and ch-1 around, rep from * around. Join with sl st to top of first ch-3. Cut yarn.

Assembly:

1 Select 1 A square and 1 B square. Hold squares right sides together. Using A or B

doubled, use a whipstitch to sew 2 squares together along 1 side. Repeat with other 2 squares.

Noro is a loosely spun single, so don't pull your stitches too hard or it will break! The felting will firm up your seams.

2 Sew these two sets together, alternating A and B squares.

3 Fold big square in half along one seam, and sew halfway up each side seam. Fold in half in the other direction, and sew halfway up each side seam.

Edging, with corner loops:

Join C at an inward point.

R1: *Sc in each st to point of square. In third ch of tch: sc, ch 8, sc in same st; rep from *, ending with sc in each st. Sl st to joining sc.

R2: *Sc in each stitch to point of square. 8 sc in chain loop; rep from *, ending with sc in each st. Sl st to joining sc. Break yarn.

Handles:

With D, chain 100. Turn. Sc in each ch.

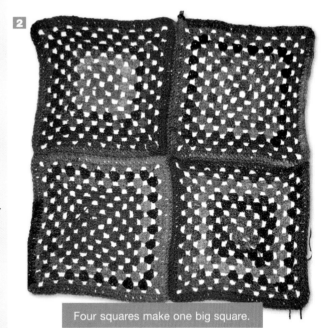

Four squares make one big square.

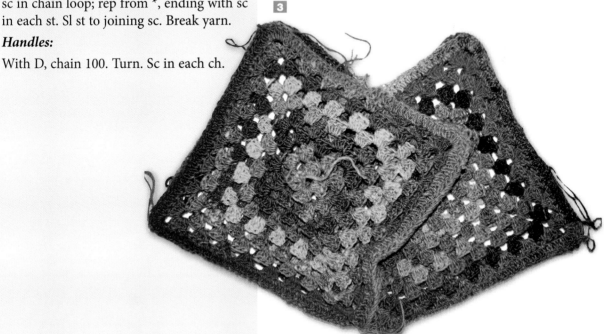

Sew the big square halfway up both side seams. It will make a pouch.

Before felting, the bag is a bit floppy.

4 ***Felting***:

Put bag and handles in a lingerie bag and felt according to directions in Chapter 2.

Assembly:

5 Thread 1 handle through 2 adjacent loops. Thread second handle through other 2 adjacent loops. Pull all 4 strings together and slide bead over all 4. Knot tops of

6 strings. Slide bead down to hold bag closed; slide up to open.

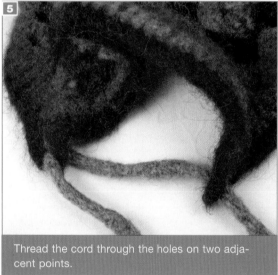

Thread the cord through the holes on two adjacent points.

Wrangle all 4 cords through the bead and knot the connected cords together.

Make It Your Own

Instead of making 4 squares, make 1 big square. Try different colors of Noro—be sure to get the Kureyon, which is all wool. You can substitute another wool; just use the hook that works with that yarn. A tiny version of this worked in crochet thread makes a lovely ornament.

Home Comforts

In This Chapter

Add a splash of color with the
Starburst Pillow

Whisk away with fun
Beachy Coasters

Get Bowled Over with these
pretty bowl projects

Dress up your table with the
Cold Mountain Table Runner

Warm up with a Soft Spiral Throw

One day, I want to own a granny square afghan. But I'm terrified that I'll
die of ennui before I finish all those squares. Here you'll find projects you
can start—and finish! And the modern edge of these projects will have
your visitors marveling that you crocheted them! They'll be especially
Bowled Over by the bowls, and you can further wow them by tucking a
Beachy Coaster under their icy drinks next to the Cold Mountain Table
Runner. Then, afterward, you can tuck up under the Soft Spiral Throw
with your head atop the Starburst Pillow. *Ahhh!*

This pillow adds a pink punch to a couch or chair with its *Jetsons*-like clustered spikes. The colors are luscious, and the cover is removable if it ever needs a bit of sprucing up. The lush yarn works up in a jiffy, too.

This Starburst Pillow will be a topic of conversation.

Starburst Pillow

Don't let the spikes on this pillow intimidate you. As you'll see, they're easy enough to create. Grab your hook and yarn, and let's go:

With A, ch 43.

R1: Hdc in 4th ch from hook and across (40 sts). Turn.

R2–4: Ch 2. Hdc across.

R5: Join B (do not cut A). Ch 2. Hdc in 1st 4 st. *Over next st, work starburst: insert hook at 5 points (see the following figure), each time drawing up loop to level of row being worked:
1 2 st to the right 1 row down,
2 1 st to right 2 rows down,
3 directly below 3 rows down,
4 1 st to left 2 rows down,
5 2 st to left 1 row down. Draw all loops up (there are 6 loops on hook), insert hook in next st, yo, and pull through all 7 loops on hook. Hdc in next 7 st. Rep from * hdc in last 3 st. Turn.

Note where the star points are—this is where you insert the hook.

Skill level:

III

Yarn:

Lamb's Pride Bulky (85% wool, 15% mohair, 113 g, 125 yd.), 1 skein Pink 105 (A); Manos del Uruguay (100% wool, 100 g, 138 yd.), Mulled Wine 118 (B); Rowan Magpie (100% wool, 100 g, 140 m) 1 skein 314 (C)

Crochet hook:

L (8mm), K (6.5mm) (K is used only for seaming.)

Notions:

Tapestry needle
Sewing needle
Thread
4 (1-inch) buttons, pink or your choice
Scrap of fleece or felt, about 2 inches square
18×10½-inch pillow form

Finished size:

18 inches wide by 10½ inches tall

Gauge:

Half-double crochet 8 stitches and 8 rows equals 4 inches

Insert the hook in these five spots to create the starburst design.

First insert the hook 2 stitches to the right and 1 row down.

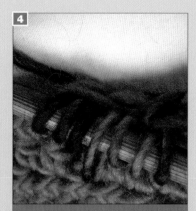

Pull all the loops up to the current row, and draw a loop through the stitch.

Yarn over and pull through all 7 loops on the hook.

To form the buttonhole, chain 2, skip 2 stitches, and half-double crochet in the next stitch.

R6–8: Ch 2. Hdc in each st across.

R9: Carry A up the side and rejoin. Hdc in next 8 st. *Over next stitch, work Starburst. Hdc in next 7 st. rep from * to end. Turn.

R10–12: Ch 2. Hdc in each stitch across.

R13: Carry B up the side and rejoin. Repeat row 5.

R14–16: Ch. 2. Hdc in each st across.

R17: Carry A up the side and rejoin. Repeat Row 9.

R18–21: Hdc across. (*Note:* 4 rows here instead of 3.)

R22: Join C. With the wrong side facing you, and *working in front loop only,* hdc across. Turn.

Crocheting through the front loop (on the wrong side) creates a sharp edge to the front so the back of the pillow doesn't show on the front.

R23–33: Ch 2. Hdc across.

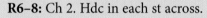 **R34:** (forming buttonhole) Ch 2, hdc in 7 st, *ch 2, sk 2 sts, hdc in 6 st, rep from * to end. Turn.

R35: Ch 2. Hdc in every st and each ch across (40 sts). Cut yarn.

Bottom back of pillow:

R1: At bottom edge, and with the wrong side facing you, join A in rightmost starting ch. Hdc in each ch across (40 sts). Cut yarn.

R2: With wrong side facing you, join C. *Working in front loop only,* work hdc across (40 sts). Turn.

R3–13: Ch 2. Hdc in each st across.

Cut yarn. Weave in ends.

Overlap buttonhole band over bottom part of pillow. Mark placement for buttons, and sew on buttons. To sew the button on securely, place a bit of fleece or felt on the opposite side of the crocheted fabric and sew the button on through both the crochet fabric and the fleece. **7**

If your buttonhole stretches and becomes too large for your button, use matching yarn to nip in the buttonhole with a small stitch or 2.

To assemble, with right sides together, turn the buttonhole band down, folding it along the edge of the pillow. Turn the button band up, folding along the edge and overlapping the buttonhole band by 2 rows (it seems wrong, but trust me here). Pin along the sides. **8**

With K hook and A yarn, sl st along seams, being sure to work through all 3 layers. Cut yarn. Weave in ends. Turn right side out, slip over pillow form, and button on. **9**

Make It Your Own

Feel free to substitute another bulky yarn when working this pillow, but remember to check your gauge! To fit another size pillow, increase the number of repeats as necessary. To make it wider, increase in increments of 8 stitches. To make it taller, add more rows in 4-row pattern repeats.

7 Sew on the button through both the crocheted fabric and the backing fabric.

8 Overlap the back sections, with the button side on top. Pin along the seam.

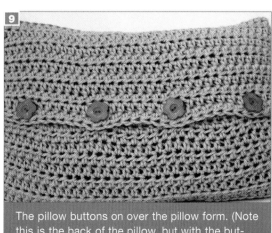

9 The pillow buttons on over the pillow form. (Note this is the back of the pillow, but with the buttons, it's almost as pretty as the front side with the starbursts!)

These coasters in multicolored hues go with just about any décor, whether your house is on the beach or completely landlocked. The fiber is both colorful and functional, with wool that sops up soda sweat. They're super-speedy to make, so you can whip them up for presents—deliver them in a little sand bucket.

The Beachy Coasters.

Beachy Coasters

You'll notice on these coasters that I call for you to work in the back loop. This accentuates the shape of the stitches. See Chapter 2 if you need a refresher.

Scallop Coaster

The scallop coaster.

With A, ch 4.

R1: In fourth ch from hook, work 6 dc (7 dc, including tch). Turn.

R2: Ch 3. Sk first st. Working in back loop only, dc in next 2 sts, 3 dc in next st, dc in next 2 sts and in tch (9 dc, including tch). Turn.

R3: Ch 3. Sk first st. Working in back loop only, dc in next 3 sts, 3 dc in next st, dc in next 3 sts and in tch (11 dc, including tch). Turn.

R4: Ch 3. Sk first st. Working in back loop only, dc in next 4 sts, 3 dc in next st, dc in next 4 sts and in tch (13 dc, including tch). Turn.

Skill level:
///

Yarn:

Lion Brand Landscapes (50% wool, 50% acrylic, 50 g, 55 yd.), 1 ball each in Autumn Trails 275 (A), Rose Garden 271 (B), Summer Fields 276 (C), and Raspberry Patch 540 (D)

Crochet hook:

K (6.5mm)

Notions:

Tapestry needle

Finished size:

About 5 inches in diameter

Gauge:

Double crochet 3 rows equals 2½ inches

R5: Ch 3. Sk first st. Working in back loop only, dc in next 6 sts, 3 dc in next st, dc in next 5 sts and in tch (15 dc, including tch). Turn.

R6: Ch 3. Sk first st. Working in back loop only, dc in next 7 sts, 3 dc in next st, dc in next 6 sts and in tch (17 dc, including tch). Turn.

R7: Ch 3. Sk first st. Working in back loop only, dc in next 7 sts, 3 dc in next st, dc in next 7 sts and in tch (19 dc, including tch).

Break off yarn. Weave in ends.

Nautilus Coaster

The nautilus coaster.

With B, ch 4. Make a sl st in first chain.

R1: 8 sc into ring. Continue in spiral, *working in back loop only:* (2 hdc in next st) 5 times, (2 dc in next st) 9 times, (2 tr in next st) 7 times, (1 tr in next st, 2 tr in next st) 8 times, 1 tr in next stitch.

Fasten off. Weave in ends.

When working a continuous spiral, there's no need to mark the beginning of the row.

Sun Coaster

Sun coaster.

With C, ch 4.

R1: In single top loop of fourth ch from hook, work 11 dc. Pull tail to tighten center of circle. Join to top of ch-3 with sl st (12 sts, including tch).

If you forgot since Chapter 2: to make a circle, join each round into a circle with a slip stitch. With small projects, you might not need to mark the first stitch.

R2: Ch 3. 1 dc in top of ch-3, 2 dc in each st around (24 sts, including tch). Join to top of ch-3 with sl st.

R3: Ch 3. *2 dc in first st, 1 dc in next st, repeat from * around, ending with 2 dc in final st. Join to top of ch-3 with sl st (36 sts). Break off yarn.

Fringe:

Cut 36 (4-inch) lengths of yarn. Fold in half, and use your crochet hook to pull the loop through the edge stitch. Pull the ends through the loop, and tug gently to snug it up. Repeat in every stitch around sun.

Starfish Coaster

Starfish coaster.

With D, ch 4.

R1: In fourth ch from hook, work 9 dc. Join to ch-3 with sl st (10 dc, including ch-3). Do not turn.

R2: Ch 3. *3 dc in next dc, 1 dc in next dc, rep from * end 1 dc in last dc. Join to ch-3 with sl st (21 sts, including ch-3). Do not turn.

R3: Ch 3. 1 dc in next 2 dc *2 dc in next dc, 1 dc in next 3 dc. Rep from *, end 1 dc in final dc. Join to ch-3 with sl st (25 dc, including ch-3).

R4: (first ray) Ch 3. Hdc in next dc, dc in next dc, dc decrease in next 2 dc (wrap yarn, pull the loop through first st, pull loop through first 2 loops on hook, wrap, insert hook in next st and pull up loop, wrap and pull loop through first 2 loops on hook, wrap and pull loop through all 3 loops on hook). Turn.

Double crochet decrease over 2 stitches.

R5: Ch 3. 3-st dc dec. (Work as for 2-st dec; then wrap and insert hook in 3rd st, pull up loop; then pull loop through first 2 loops on hook, wrap, and pull loop through all 4 loops on hook.) Break off yarn.

Rejoin yarn with sl st in next dc on circle. Work as for first ray.

Repeat until 5 rays are completed.

To finish, weave in ends. At tip of ray, thread yarn end through all 4 loops again to tighten.

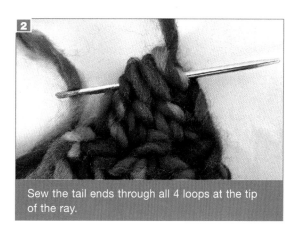

Sew the tail ends through all 4 loops at the tip of the ray.

Make It Your Own

Use any absorbent, thick yarn for these coasters. Or if you like one coaster better than the others, make a set of suns, for example, in different colors.

Crochet is especially well suited to bowls because it produces a very stable fabric (with knitting, you'd have to felt it to make it this sturdy). Although these bowls look very different from one another, they all have the same basic parts: a circular base, tubular sides, and an edge. Bowls 1 and 3 decrease to form a lip, and bowl 2 increases to create a wavy edge.

These three bowls won't stay empty for long.

Bowled Over!

See each project for materials

Edged Bowl / / /

Wavy Bowl / / /

Bird Nest Bowl / / /

Some notes before you begin:

- To make the bowls sturdy, use a hook 1 or 2 sizes smaller than what the yarn label recommends.
- The bowls are crocheted in a circle with the right side facing you. You do not turn after the rows.
- Clip a row marker at the first stitch of each row to help you keep track.
- Use a sliding loop to start the circles so you don't have a hole in the center of your bowl. To do it, chain 2, work stitches in the second chain from the hook and then pull the tail to tighten the hole.

The sliding loop. After crocheting the given number of stitches, tug on the tail to pull the loop into a little bitty hole.

Edged Bowl

The complementary color yarn really pops on this Edged Bowl.

Skill level:

/ / /

Yarn:

Manos del Uruguay (100% wool, 100 g, 138 yd.), Eclipse 111 (A); Lamb's Pride Bulky (85% wool, 15% mohair, 113 g, 125 yd.), 1 skein Rosado Rose 183 (B)

Crochet hook:

K (6.5mm), H (5mm)

Notions:

Tapestry needle

Finished size:

6-inch base, 8 inches at widest diameter, 3 inches deep

Gauge:

18 rows and 15 stitches equals 4 inches

The Manos del Uruguay arrives in a skein, so you'll have to wind it in a ball. Because it's loosely spun, it's happiest being wound by hand, rather than on a ball winder.

R1: With A, make a loop. In it, sc 6. Join with sl. st. to first sc.

R2: 2 sc in each sc. Join with sl st to first sc (12 sc).

R3: *1 sc in first sc, 2 sc in next sc. Rep from * around. Join with sl st to first sc (18 sc).

R4: *1 sc in next 2 sc, 2 sc in next sc. Rep from * around. Join with sl st to first sc (24 sc).

R5: *1 sc in next 3 sc, 2 sc in next sc. Rep from * around. Join with sl st to first sc (30 sc).

R6: *1 sc in next 4 sc, 2 sc in next sc. Rep from * around. Join with sl st to first sc (36 sc).

R7: *1 sc in next 5 sc, 2 sc in next sc. Rep from * around. Join with sl st to first sc (42 sc).

R8: *1 sc in next 6 sc, 2 sc in next sc. Rep from * around. Join with sl st to first sc (48 sc).

R9: *1 sc in next 7 sc, 2 sc in next sc. Rep from * around. Join with sl st to first sc (54 sc).

R10: *1 sc in next 8 sc, 2 sc in next sc. Rep from * around. Join with sl st to first sc (60 sc).

R11: *1 sc in next 9 sc, 2 sc in next sc. Rep from * around. Join with sl st to first sc (66 sc).

R12: *1 sc in next 10 sc, 2 sc in next sc. Rep from * around. Join with sl st to first sc (72 sc).

R13–22: Sc in each sc around. Join with sl st to first sc (72 sc).

R23: *Sc 2 tog, sc 10, rep from * around (66 sc).

R24: *Sc 2 tog, sc 9, rep from * around (60 sc).

R25: *Sc 2 tog, sc 8, rep from * around (54 sc).

R26: Sc around (54 sc).

Break off yarn.

1 With B yarn and K hook, work crab stitch around the top edge.

Crab stitch is single crochet worked in the reverse direction (left to right). (See Chapter 12 for more details.)

Wavy Bowl

Have some fun with this Wavy Bowl.

Skill Level:

/ / /

Yarn:

Lamb's Pride Bulky (85% wool, 15% mohair, 113 g, 125 yd.), 1 skein Rosado Rose 183

Crochet hook:

K (6.5mm)

Notions:

Tapestry needle
9 beaded stitch markers (optional; you can string beads on instead of using the stitch markers. You'll need 9 to 18 beads, along with heavy thread)

Finished size:

4½-inch base, 6½ at widest diameter, 2½ inches deep

Gauge:

14 rows and 13 stitches for 4 inches

Beaded stitch markers add a little more sparkle to the waves in this bowl.

R1: Make a loop. In it, sc 6. Join with sl. st. to first sc.

R2: 2 sc in each sc. Join with sl st to first sc (12 sc).

R3: *1 sc in first sc, 2 sc in next sc. rep from * around. Join with sl st to first sc (18 sc).

R4: *1 sc in next 2 sc, 2 sc in next sc. Rep from * around. Join with sl st to first sc (24 sc).

R5: *1 sc in next 3 sc, 2 sc in next sc. Rep from * around. Join with sl st to first sc (30 sc).

R6: *1 sc in next 4 sc, 2 sc in next sc. Rep from * around. Join with sl st to first sc (36 sc).

R7: *1 sc in next 5 sc, 2 sc in next sc. Rep from * around. Join with sl st to first sc (42 sc).

R8–15: Sc in each sc around. Join with sl st to first sc (42 sc).

R16: 2 sc in each sc around (84 sc).

R17: 2 sc in each sc around (168 sc).

Break off yarn. Weave in ends.

To embellish, hang beaded stitch markers on the outer edge of each ripple or sew beads to the outer edge.

Wavy from above is groovy.

Bird Nest Bowl

The shape and texture of this Bird Nest Bowl give it its name.

Skill level:

/ / /

Yarn:

1 skein recycled silk scrap yarn (I scored my yarn at a farmers' market in Los Angeles. See Appendix B for a silk yarn resource.)

Crochet hook:

K

Notions:

Tapestry needle
Ribbons
15 to 20 beads in various sizes, from 1mm to 15mm
Thread
Sewing needle

Finished size:

5-inch base, 7½ inches at widest diameter, 2½ inches deep

Gauge:

14 stitches and 14 rows equals 4 inches

 It can be pesky to try to find your stitches with the silk yarn. Be sure to place a marker at the beginning of the round and keep track of the number of rows in this highly textured stuff.

R1: Make a loop. In it, sc 6. Join with sl. st. to first sc.

R2: 2 sc in each sc. Join with sl st to first sc (12 sc).

R3: *1 sc in 1st sc, 2 sc in next sc. Rep from * around. Join with sl st to first sc (18 sc).

Slip the bead through the loop and adjust as you like.

Sew on the beads and baubles as you like.

R4: *1 sc in next 2 sc, 2 sc in next sc. Rep from * around. Join with sl st to first sc (24 sc).

R5: *1 sc in next 3 sc, 2 sc in next sc. Rep from * around. Join with sl st to first sc (30 sc).

R6: *1 sc in next 4 sc, 2 sc in next sc. Rep from * around. Join with sl st to first sc (36 sc).

R7: *1 sc in next 5 sc, 2 sc in next sc. Rep from * around. Join with sl st to first sc (42 sc).

R8: *1 sc in next 6 sc, 2 sc in next sc. Rep from * around. Join with sl st to first sc (48 sc).

R9–14: Sc in each sc around. Join with sl st to first sc (48 sc).

R15: *Sc 2 tog, sc 5, rep from * around (42 sc).

R16: *Sc 2 tog, sc 4, rep from * around (36 sc).

R17: *Sc 2 tog, sc 3, rep from * around (30 sc).

R18: Sc around.

To keep track of the number of rows, try this trick: set 10 paper clips on your work table. As you finish each row, put a paper clip into a container.

1. To embellish, cut 10 to 15 (4- to 6-inch)
2. lengths of ribbon. Fold a piece in half and use your crochet hook to pull the loop through the bowl. Pull the ends through the loop, and pull taut. Add beads and baubles as desired.

Make It Your Own

You can vary the size of the bowl to suit your needs. You could make shallow bowls by doing more increases for the base and fewer rows in the side. Make deep bowls by crocheting more rows on the side. Make a tall, skinny vase by doing fewer increases and many more rows on the sides.

Cold Mountain Table Runner

This table runner, inspired by Charles Frazier's novel *Cold Mountain,* is an adaptation of the Moon over the Mountain quilt pattern. The block is constructed in three parts, starting with a triangle for the mountain.

Dress up your table with this Cold Mountain Table Runner.

Skill level:

111

Yarn:

Araucania Nature Wool (100% wool, 100 g, 240 yd.), 1 skein each color 112 (A), 103 (B), 120 (C); Lamb's Pride Bulky (85% wool, 15% mohair, 113 g, 125 yd.), 1 skein Sun Yellow 13 (D); Manos del Uruguay (100% wool, 100 g, 138 yd.), 1 skein each Marigold 58 (E), Rose O (F), Magenta S (G), Autumn 106 (H)

Crochet hook:

N (10mm), K (6.5mm)

Notions:

Tapestry needle

Finished size:

Block: 11 inches wide by 10 inches tall
Runner: 11 inches by 60 inches

Gauge:

Double crochet 12 stitches and 6 rows equals 4 inches

Make 6 mountains, 2 in each color.

Mountain

(Make 6, 2 each in A, B, and C.)

Using N hook, ch 4.

R1: In fourth chain from hook, hdc 2. Turn.

R2: Ch 2, 2 hdc in first st, 1 hdc in next st, 2 hdc in top of ch-3 (5 hdc). Turn.

R3: Ch 2, 2 hdc in first st, hdc in next 3 st, 2 hdc in final st (7 hdc). Turn.

R4: Ch 2, 2 hdc in first st, hdc in next 5 st, 2 hdc in final st (9 hdc). Turn.

R5: Ch 2, 2 hdc in first st, hdc in next 7 st, 2 hdc in final st (11 hdc). Turn.

R6: Ch 2, 2 hdc in first st, hdc in next 9 st, 2 hdc in final st (13 hdc). Turn.

R7: Ch 2, 2 hdc in first st, hdc in next 11 st, 2 hdc in final st (15 hdc). Turn.

R8: Ch 2, 2 hdc in first st, hdc in next 13 st, 2 hdc in final st (17 hdc). Turn.

R9: Ch 2, 2 hdc in first st, hdc in next 15 st, 2 hdc in final st (19 hdc). Turn.

R10: Ch 2, 2 hdc in first st, hdc in next 17 st, 2 hdc in final st (21 hdc). Turn.

R11: Ch 2, 2 hdc in first st, hdc in next 19 st, 2 hdc in final st (23 hdc). Turn.

R12: Ch 2, 2 hdc in first st, hdc in next 21 st, 2 hdc in final st (25 hdc).

Cut yarn. Weave in ends.

To block triangles, mist with steam iron and then pin to a board to 12 inches along the base and 6 inches from the center of the base to the tip.

1 Block triangles to 12 inches along the base and 6 inches from peak to center of base.

Remember, when blocking, do not touch the iron to the fabric. When you have your piece pinned, lightly mist with water, and hold the steam iron about 1 inch over your crochet fabric.

Sun

(Make 1 each of D and E for each color of mountain.)

R1: With K hook, join yarn with sl st in peak of mountain. (This is actually the starting point of the triangle.) Ch 3. Work 9 dc in starting ch (10 sts including ch-3). Join with sl st to single loop of row 2 mountain. Turn.

R2: Ch 3. 1 dc in first st, 2 dcs in each st around, 2 dc in top of tch. (20 sts, including ch-3). Join with sl st to single loop of row 4 of mountain. Turn.

R3: Ch 3. 1 dc in first st, *2 dc in next st, 1 dc in next st, rep from *. 1 dc in final st (30 sts, including ch-3). Join with sl st to single loop of row 6 of mountain. Turn.

R4: Ch 3. 1 dc in first st, *2 dc in next stitch, 1 dc in next 2 sts, rep from *. 1 dc in final st (39 sts, including ch-3). Join with sl st to single loop of row 8 of mountain. Turn.

Break off yarn, leaving a 10-inch tail. Use the tail to whipstitch the sun to the mountain on the back side of the block.

Join the sun to the mountain with slip stitch in the top loop of the mountain.

Join the edge of the sun to the mountain with a slip stitch.

The right side of the sun has little V's around the edge.

Whipstitch the sun to the mountain, through a single loop on the mountain.

Sky

(Make 2 each of F, G, and H.)

With the right side of the sun facing you, and with K hook, join yarn at the right base of the sun, leaving a 10-inch tail.

Turning a circle into a square will make you feel like a wizard. The side of the first row includes single crochets, and the corners will have varying combinations of double and triple crochets—so you'll have to pay attention!

R1: *Working in back loop only,* sc in first 8 sts, hdc in next 2 sts, sk 2 sts, in next st (1 tr, 2 dc, ch 2, 2 dc, 1 tr), sk next 2 sts, hdc in next 2 sts, sc in next 5 sts, hdc in next 2 sts, sk 2 sts, in next st (1 tr, 2 dc, ch 2, 2 dc, 1 tr), sk 2 sts, hdc in next 2 sts, 2 sc in last 8 sts. Join with sl st to single loop of mountain. Turn.

R2: Ch 3. Working in both loops (here and throughout), 2 dc in first st. 1 dc in next 12 sts, in corner ch-2 space (1 dc, 1 tr, ch 2, 1 tr, 1 dc), 1 dc in next 15 sts, in corner ch-2 space (1 dc, 1 tr, ch 2, 1 tr, 1 dc), dc in next 12 sts, 2 dc in final st. Join with sl st to single loop of mountain. Turn.

R3: Ch 3. 2 dc in first st. 1 dc in next 15 sts, in corner ch-2 space (2 dc, ch 2, 2 dc), 1 dc in next 19 sts, in corner ch-2 space (2 dc, ch 2, 2 dc), dc in next 15 sts, 2 dc in final sts. Join with sl st to single loop of mountain. Turn.

R4: Ch 3. 2 dc in first st. 1 dc in next 18 sts, in corner ch-2 space (2 dc, ch 2, 2 dc), 1 dc in next 23 sts, in corner ch-2 space (2 dc, ch 2, 2 dc), dc in next 12 sts, 2 dc in final st. Join with sl st to single loop of mountain. Turn.

R5: Ch 3. 2 dc in first st. 1 dc in next 21 sts, 5 dc in corner ch-2 space, 1 dc in next 27 sts, 5 dc in corner ch-2 space, dc in next 21 sts, 2 dc in final st. Join with sl st to single loop of mountain. Turn.

Using the tails, whipstitch the sky to the mountain on the back of the square.

Block the squares to 12×12 inches. Lay out the squares before you sew them together. Move them around until you find an arrangement that makes you happy. Whipstitch squares together to make 2 strips of 3 blocks. Sew the 2 strips together at the mountain end, so the mountains point to opposite ends of the table.

At the center, connect 2 strips of 3 blocks at the mountain end.

Make It Your Own

Substitute yarns as you like, but be sure to check gauge. You can use 2 squares to make a pillow (or 1 square, with fabric on the back of the pillow) or make lots more squares to make a blanket.

Soft Spiral Throw

The afternoon yawns before you. You could read a book, sip some tea, write a poem—or just slip this bit of a frothy throw over you and nap a bit. The whimsical spiral pattern in this throw lends itself to happy daydreams.

Cuddle up with the Soft Spiral Throw.

Skill level:
11

Yarn:
Moonlight Mohair (35% mohair, 30% acrylic, 25% cotton, 10% polyester metallic, 50 g, 82 yd.), 6 balls Glacier Bay 205 (A), 2 balls Safari 203 (B)

Crochet hook:
P (11.5mm)

Notions:
Tapestry needle
Stitch marker

Finished size:
60 inches in diameter

Gauge:
Double crochet 6 stitches and 4 rows equals 4 inches

This yarn is very pesky to uncrochet—the mohair fibers want to grab on to one another—so count carefully! And be wary of yarn substitutions. This throw achieves its frothiness with a fluffy yarn and big hook. A sturdier yarn or smaller hook may leave you feeling like you're napping under a big potholder.

The blanket is worked in the round with the right side facing you. Do not turn at the ends of the rounds.

With A, c h 4 and join with sl st to form a ring.

R1: Ch 1, 8 sc in ring; join with sl st to first sc (8 sc). Place marker at beginning of round, and move up each round.

R2: Ch 3 (counts as first dc here and throughout), dc in same st, ch 1, (2 dc in next st, ch 1) around, join with sl st to first dc (16 sts).

R3: Sl st in first dc, ch 3, dc in same st and in ch-1 sp, ch 2, sk next dc *2 dc in next dc, dc in next ch-1 space, ch 2, sk next st. Rep from * around. Join with sl st to first dc (24 sts).

R4: Sl st in next dc, ch 3, 2 dc in next dc, dc in next ch-2 space, ch 2, sk next dc *dc in next dc, 2 dc in next dc, dc in next ch-2 space, ch 2, sk next st. Rep from * around. Join with sl st to first dc (32 dc).

After a few rows, put a marker (or tie a piece of contrasting yarn) on the front side. That way, you won't have to think too hard about which side is up.

R5: Sl st in next dc, ch 3, dc in next dc, 2 dc in next dc, dc in next ch-2 space, ch 3, sk next dc *dc in next 2 dc, 2 dc in next dc, dc in next ch-2 space, ch 3, sk next st. Rep from * around. Join with sl st to first dc (40 dc).

R6–7: Sl st in next dc, ch 3 *dc in next dc and in each dc across to last dc of section. 2 dc in this dc, dc in ch-3 space, ch 3, sk next st. Rep from * around. Join with sl st to first dc.

When you join a new ball of A, just tie it to the end of the spent ball with an overhand knot. The fuzzy yarn will absorb the ends.

R8: Sl st in next dc, ch 3 *dc in next dc and in each dc across to last dc of section. 2 dc in this dc, dc in ch-3 space, ch 4, sk next st. Rep from * around. Join with sl st to first dc.

R9–11: Sl st in next dc, ch 3 *dc in next dc and in each dc across to last dc of section. 2 dc in this dc, dc in ch-4 space, ch 4, sk next st. Rep from * around. Join with sl st to first dc.

R12: Sl st in next dc, ch 3 *dc in next dc and in each dc across to last dc of section. 2 dc in this dc, dc in ch-4 space, ch 5, sk next st. Rep from * around. Join with sl st to first dc.

R13–16: Sl st in next dc, ch 3 *dc in next dc and in each dc across to last dc of section. 2 dc in this dc, dc in ch-5 space, ch 5, sk next st. Rep from * around. Join with sl st to first dc.

R17: Sl st in next dc, ch 3 *dc in next dc and in each dc across to last dc of section. 2 dc in this dc, dc in ch-5 space, ch 6, sk next st. Rep from * around. Join with sl st to first dc.

R18–22: Sl st in next dc, ch 3 *dc in next dc and in each dc across to last dc of section. 2 dc in this dc, dc in ch-6 space, ch 6, sk next st. Rep from * around. Join with sl st to first dc.

R23 (1st row of edging): Join B. Ch 3. Dc in 1st dc and in each dc across to last dc of section. 2 dc in this dc. *6 dc across 6-chain space. Dc in every dc to last dc of section. 2 dc in this dc. Rep from * to end. Join with sl st to starting ch-3.

R24: *Ch 3. Join with sl st to next st, and rep from * around. Join with sl st to first st.

Cut yarn. Weave in ends.

Jewelry and Other Adornments

In This Chapter

Decorate your neck with a
Jewel Box Necklace

Rockin' Wrist Wraps—
the name says it all

Keep it close with a
Dotty Choker

Make fun, fast adornments for yourself and others. The Jewel Box
Necklace is super easy and adds a touch of glam to any outfit, from a
white T-shirt to a little black dress. And for the rockers in your life,
Rockin' Wrist Wraps are just the thing—my preteen kids love them!
The Dotty Choker looks complex but is very simple, and you can
adapt it to not only necklaces, but also bracelets, anklets—even pet
collars!

This gem is so simple it will make you blush—almost as much as when people compliment you on your lovely strand of jewels. As you chain it, the railroad-style ribbon yarn forms tiny boxes of color.

When you see how easy this necklace is, you'll want to make several in different lengths.

Jewel Box Necklace

Chain necklaces *loosely* to desired length.

Cut yarn and pull through the last loop. Tie the two ends together in a double knot. Then tie another double knot.

Cut ends ¼ inch from knot.

The ribbon sparkles and is sure to catch many an eye.

Make It Your Own

Trellis comes in different colors, so you can make a necklace in each to match each of your outfits! Also, consider other uses for the chain: bracelet, anklet, ribbon to wrap a present, or a long chain for a holiday garland! What else can you think of?

Skill level:
/ / /

Yarn:
Lion Brand Trellis (100% nylon, 50 g, 115 yd.), 1 ball Pastel Garden 306

Crochet hook:
K (Aluminum is best. Bamboo, wood, or acrylic might catch on the yarn.)

Finished size:
30 inches long; 24 inches long

Gauge:
Varies

This gang of wrist decorations is simply addictive, and you'll have them wrapped up in no time. The suedelike yarn is super soft. You need just a bit to make each wrap, so pool your yarn stash with your friends for more colors.

Make a variety of wraps.

Rockin' Wrist Wraps

Braid Wrist Wrap

As the name suggests, the Braid Wrist Wrap is made of 3 chains braided together.

Skill level:
///

Yarn:
Lion Brand Lion Suede (100% polyester, 85 g, 122 yd.), 1 ball each Spice 133 (A), Vineyard 202 (B), Eggplant 147 (C)

Crochet hook:
J (6mm)

Notions:
Tapestry needle

Finished size:
½ inches wide by 6½ inches long (without tie)

Gauge:
12 chains equals 4 inches

These wraps are designed to fit a 6- to 6½-inch wrist. To make them longer, simply add more chains for the Braid, Fringe, and Edge Wrist Wraps. For the Spike Wrist Wrap, you must add 4 chains to make a complete pattern repeat; if you need fewer, just add another single crochet at the ends of the red row. For the Wave Wrist Wrap, single crochet rows across the short ends to make it longer.

The wraps are smaller than a gauge swatch, so just do this to measure: after the first row is done, wrap the piece around your wrist and see how it fits.

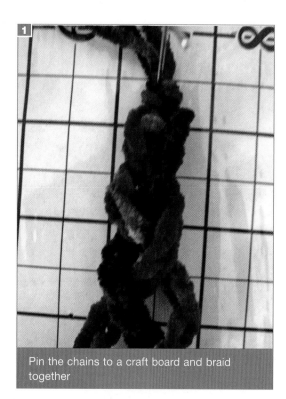

Pin the chains to a craft board and braid together

Leaving a 10-inch tail, with A, ch 23. Cut, leaving another 10-inch tail, and pull the end through the last ch.

Repeat with colors B and C.

Holding the 3 chains together, tie an overhand knot close to one end of the chains. Tie to a doorknob, or pin the knot to a craft board. Braid the chains together, and tie an overhand knot close to the end of the braided chains. Have a friend knot it onto your wrist. Cut the yarn ends to the desired length.

Make It Your Own

Crochet beads into the braid. Add them to the yarn before you start crocheting and work them in as you like.

Edge Wrist Wrap

The fuchsia pops in the brown of this Edge Wrist Wrap.

Skill level:
///

Yarn:
Lion Brand Lion Suede (100% polyester, 85 g, 122 yd.): 1 ball each Coffee 126 (A), Fuchsia 146 (B)

Crochet hook:
J (6mm)

Notions:
Tapestry needle

Finished size:
1½ inches wide by 7½ inches long

Gauge:
11 double crochets equals
4 inches

With A, ch 23.

R1: In fourth chain from hook, work dc, then dc across (21 dc, including ch-3).

R2: Do not turn. Join B with a sl st, and work crab stitch: sc *in front loop* of last dc worked. Then sc in dc to right. Continue across, working from left to right, ending with sc in top of ch-3.

Work the fuchsia in the front loop only.

Join the brown chain with a slip stitch at the corner of one end and then single crochet back along the loop.

Crab stitch (also called reverse single crochet) is usually an edging stitch. When it's working within the fabric, you must work in the front loop only, because the finished stitch does not leave a working base. You do the next row in the back loop.

R3: Cut A and rejoin at right side of work. Ch 3. Working in back loop of first row of dc, dc across (21 sts, including ch-3). Cut yarn and pull through last st.

Using a tapestry needle, weave in ends.

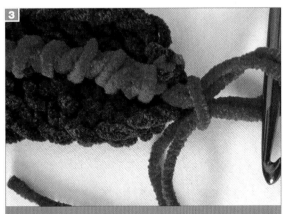

Pull the fuchsia loop through and then pull the ends through the loop.

With the wrong side facing you, join A at right corner of one short end. Ch 5. Join
2 with sl st to the other corner of the end. Sc back around the ch-5 loop. Join with sl st to the other corner of the end. Cut a 12-inch length of B. Fold in half, and pull the loop through the center of the opposite short side, in line with the stripe. Pull the
3 ends of the yarn through the loop.

4 To wear, pull one end of B through the loop and tie to the other end.

Make It Your Own

For more sparkle, add beads to the ends of the ties.

To fasten, pull the fuchsia loop through the brown loop and tie.

Fringe Wrist Wrap

This Fringe Wrist Wrap has a very retro Western feel.

Skill level:
///

Yarn:
Lion Brand Lion Suede (100% polyester, 85 g, 122 yd.), 1 ball each Desert 200 (A), Mocha 125 (B)

Crochet hook:
J (6mm)

Notions:
Tapestry needle

Finished size:
1½ inches wide by 7 inches long

Gauge:
11 single crochets equals 4 inches

Fringe stitch is worked from the back so the loop appears on the front. You later cut the loops to make the fringe.

With A, ch 21.

R1: Sc in second ch from your hook and across (20 sts).

R2: Join B and turn. Do a loop st: insert your hook into st as usual. Use the index finger of your free hand to form a loop about 1 inch long. Pick up both strands of the loop, and draw them through. Wrap yarn over hook (as for a regular sc), and pull through all 3 loops on hook. Repeat in each stitch across (20 sts).

R3: Cut A and rejoin with ch. Ch 2. Dc across (20 sts).

R4: Repeat row 2.

R5: Repeat row 3. Cut yarn and pull through last loop.

Weave in ends. Snip the center of each loop to create the fringe. Cut 2 (12-inch) pieces of each yarn. Hold one of each together and fold in half. Loop through the center of one short end to create a tie. Repeat on the other short end. To wear, tie the ends together.

For a loop stitch, use the index finger of your free hand to form a loop and then finish the single crochet.

Spike Wrist Wrap

Red energizes black in this Spike Wrist Wrap.

Skill level:
///

Yarn:
Lion Brand Lion Suede (100% polyester, 85 g, 122 yd.), 1 ball each Ebony 153 (A), Scarlet 113 (B)

Crochet hook:
J (6mm)

Notions:
Tapestry needle
1 (¾ inch) black or red button

Finished size:
2 inches wide by 7 inches long

Gauge:
11 single crochets equals 4 inches

With A, ch 21.

R1: Sc in second ch from hook and in each ch across (20 sc).

R2–3: Ch 1, turn. Sc in each st across (20 sc).

R4: Join B. Sc in first 2 sc. *Do spike st: insert hook 2 rows down and 1 row to

the left; pull hook up to make loop even with row; yo and pull through both loops on hook. Sk sc spike st was worked over.

1. Sc in next 2 sc. Do spike st: insert hook in same hole as previous spike st; draw up, yo, and pull through both loops on hook. Sk sc spike st was worked over. Sc in next 2 sc. Rep from * to end.

R5: Cut A and rejoin. Sc in each st across (20 sc).

R6: Ch 1, turn. Sc in each st across (20 sc).

Cut yarn. Weave in ends.

2. With the wrong side facing you, join B at the center of one short end, matching to red stripe. Ch 5. Join with sl st at same place B is joined. Sew a button to the center of the other short end.

To do the spike stitch, insert your hook 2 rows down and 1 row to the left.

To wear, wrap the red loop around a black velvet button.

Wave Wrist Wrap

Do the wave!—Wave Wrist Wrap, that is.

Skill level:
///

Yarn:
Lion Brand Lion Suede (100% polyester, 85 g, 122 yd.), 1 ball each Teal 178 (A), Olive 132 (B), Fuchsia 146 (C), Spice 133 (D), Eggplant 147 (E)

Crochet hook:
J (6mm)

Notions:
Tapestry needle
1 (¾- to 1-inch) button, gold or your choice

Finished size:
3 inches wide by 8 inches tall

Gauge:
11 single crochets equals 4 inches

With A, ch 23.

R1: In second ch from hook, 2 sc *1 sc in next 4 ch, sk 2 ch, 1 sc in next 4 ch, 3 sc in next ch. Rep from *, ending with 2 sc in final ch. Turn.

R2: Join B. Ch 1, 2 sc in first st, *1 sc in next 4 st, sk 2 st, 1 sc in next 4 sc, 3 sc in next st. Rep from *, ending with 2 sc in last st. Turn.

R3: Join C. Repeat row 2.

R4: Join D. Repeat row 2.

R5: Join E. Repeat row 2.

Cut yarn. Weave in ends.

Button placket:

R1: Join C at one short end. Work 6 sc across. Turn.

R2-3: Ch 1, sc across (6 sc). Cut yarn.

Buttonhole placket:

R1: Join C at other short end. Work 6 sc across. Turn.

R2: Ch 1, sc in next 2 sc, ch 2, sk 2 sc; sc in next 2 sc. Turn.

R3: Ch 1, sc in next 2 sc, sc each ch, sc in next 2 sc (6 sts).

1 Cut yarn. Weave in ends. Sew button to center of button placket.

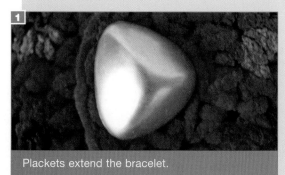

Plackets extend the bracelet.

Make It Your Own

Not a fan of these colors? Then choose the colors that rock you!

Dotty Choker

This slender choker is just the thing to add a bit of color. It makes a terrific friendship bracelet, too. Or you could do it in natural colors and add some shells or beads—the boy in your life just might like it!

Skill level:

/ / /

Yarn:
DMC 3 (100% cotton, 16.4 yd.), 1 skein each color 801 (A), color 603 (B)

Crochet hook:
1 (2.75mm) steel hook

Notions:
Tapestry needle
1 (10mm) bead, in color to coordinate with colors

Finished size:
½ inch wide by 15 inches long

Gauge:
Varies. The clasp allows you to adjust the closeness of the choker.

For when you need just a little something pretty, the Dotty Choker.

Here's the pattern stitch for the Dotty Choker.

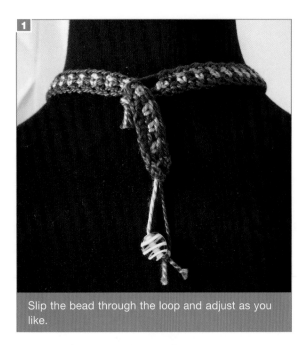

Slip the bead through the loop and adjust as you like.

Adjust the pattern a bit to make a friendship bracelet (or two or three …).

You'll work from the front only on this choker. That creates a cleaner, flatter design. And if your crochet curls as you work, switch to a larger hook.

With A, ch 94.

R1: Sc in second ch from hook, *sc in next ch, ch 1, sk 1 ch, rep from *, ending with sc in last sc. Do not turn.

R2: Join B with sl st at starting end. Sc in first sc. *Ch 1, sk 1 sc, sc in next ch-1 space, rep from *. End ch 1, sc in last sc. Do not turn.

R3: Cut A, leaving an 8-inch tail, and rejoin with sl st at starting end. Sc in first sc, *ch 1, sk 1 sc, sc in next ch-1 space. Rep from *. End ch 1, sc in last sc.

Cut yarn, leaving an 8-inch tail.

At one end, thread the bead on B. Tie a knot with A and B, securing the bead. On the other end, tie an overhand knot with A and B to create a loop. To wear, slip the bead through the loop and pull to desired closeness.

Make It Your Own

The cotton thread is cheap enough to buy a bundle and make a variety of colors. This makes an excellent friendship bracelet, also.

It's a Wrap!

In This Chapter

Take off the chill—in style!—with the
Dogwood Blossom Wrap

A Shoulder Warmer, for when
you need a little something

The Big Doily Wrap—this isn't your
grandmother's doily!

A crochet skirt? You bet: introducing the
Maximal Skirt

How many ways can you wrap a wrap? Well, at least four, as
you'll see by the projects in this chapter. Three of these wraps
are elegant variations of a rectangle, one is a circle, and they all
range from loose to close-fitting. Grab your hook and yarn, find
a project that works for you, and wrap it on!

A wrap is the perfect garment when it's just a bit cold—no sleeves to get you too warm and no extra fabric to hang around like a poncho. Evoking 1940s movie stars, this version adds instant elegance. The Calmer yarn is touch-me soft, and the airy thistles pattern is lovely to work: the stitches are worked between the stitches rather than in them, so it works up more quickly.

Add instant elegance (not to mention warmth) with this Dogwood Blossom Wrap.

Dogwood Blossom Wrap

Some patterns are suitable for yarn experimentation, but this isn't one of them. Other yarns may prove too sturdy with this pattern, creating something more like a straightjacket. Not exactly the cozy feeling you're going for with this project.

Ch 39.

R1: In fourth ch from hook, dc 1 *sk 2 ch, 5 dc into next ch, sk 2 ch, 1 dc in each of next 2 ch. Rep from * to end.

1 **R2:** Ch 3. 2 dc in first dc, sk 3 dc *1 dc in space between second and third dc of shell, 1 dc in sp between third and fourth dc of shell, sk 3 dc, 5 dc in space between 2 vertical dc, sk 3 dc, repeat from *, ending 3 dc in space between last dc and ch-3. Turn.

R3: Ch 3. 1 dc between first 2 dc, *sk 3 dc, 5 dc in space between 2 vertical dc, sk 3 dc, 1 dc in space between second and third dc of shell, 1 dc between third and fourth dc of shell, repeat from *, ending 1 dc in space between last dc and chain 3, 1 dc in third of ch-3. Turn.

1 For this pattern, you work the double crochets between the double crochet stitches of the shell on the previous row.

Skill level:

11

Yarn:

Rowan Calmer (75% cotton, 25% acrylic, 50 g, 175 yd.), 3 balls Drift 460

Crochet hook:

H (5mm)

Notions:

Tapestry needle

Finished size:

9 inches wide by 39 inches around

Gauge:

In shell stitch: 2½ shells and 8½ rows equals 4 inches

Whip stitch the ends together.

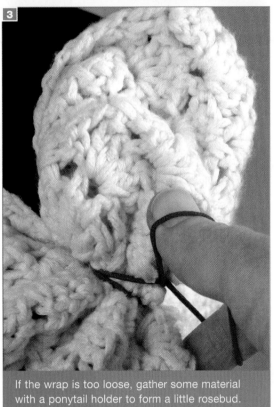

If the wrap is too loose, gather some material with a ponytail holder to form a little rosebud.

Repeat rows 2 and 3 for 38 inches.

As you near the end, have a friend wrap the wrap around you. It should be snug but not confining. It will give some with wear.

2. To finish, hold the two short ends together, and whip stitch the tops of the shells to the foundation ch to form a tube. Be sure the material isn't twisted.

3. Slip the tube over your head, and adjust over your shoulders. If the wrap is a bit loose, gather with a ponytail holder to form a little rosebud.

Make It Your Own

Use a brooch to gather the excess fabric or just as adornment if the wrap fits well. To make a Moebius wrap, which has a mysterious-looking twist in it, you can put a half-twist in the wrap before sewing the seam. Wear the wrap with the twist in front.

Shoulder Warmer

What is it with the temperature in office buildings? Too cold one minute, too hot the next. Try this shoulder warmer to ward off the chill so you can concentrate on your work. The soft ribbing drapes in the back, and the cuffs keep it in place. The bit of bling at the cuffs dresses it up, too, so if you forget to take it off when you leave work, no worries—it looks great!

Warm things up a bit with this stylish Shoulder Warmer.

Just enough coverage to take off the chill.

Skill level:
///

Yarn:
Lion Brand Homespun (98% acrylic, 2% polyester, 170 g, 185 yd.), 2 skeins Fiesta 396 (A); Rowan Calmer (75% cotton, 25% acrylic, 50 g, 175 yd.), 1 ball Coffee Bean 481 (B); Lion Brand Fun Fur (100% polyester, 50 g, 60 yd.), Olive Green 132 (C)

Crochet hook:
L, G

Notions:
Tapestry needle

Finished size:
12 inches wide by 54 inches from cuff to cuff

Gauge:
Double crochet 7 stitches and 5 rows equals 4 inches

Bring the ends together, and slip stitch into first single crochet.

With yarn A and crochet hook L, ch 82.

R1: In third ch from hook, work dc, dc across (80 sts).

R2–17: Ch 2, turn. Working in back loop only, dc in second st and across, including tch.

It's a bit tough to see the stitches in this or any highly textured yarn. Focus on the first couple stitches, lifting them to see where you are. The rest of the stitches will come more easily.

Cuffs:

R1: With yarn B and size G hook, sc across one short end of wrap. Pull two ends together and sc into first sc, making a circle. This is the cuff.

On the stretchiness scale, the woven stitch (single crochet, chain 1) is more stretchy than solid single crochet, but less stretchy than the rib stitch. It provides some stretch without giving *too* much.

R2: Sc into first sc, *ch 1, sk 1 sc, sc into next sc, rep from * around. Do not join into first sc, but keep working in a spiral.

R3–10: *Sc into ch-1 space, ch 1, rep from *.

R11: Join C. Sc in every sc and every ch-1 space. Join with sl st to first sc. Cut yarn.

Repeat on the other short side to make the second cuff.

Join C at cuff edge, and sc around cuff. Join to first sc. Cut yarn. Repeat for second cuff, being sure to fold the wrap in the same direction as you did for the first cuff.

Weave in ends.

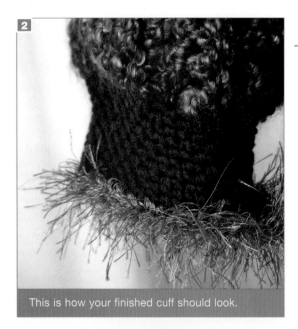

This is how your finished cuff should look.

Make It Your Own

If you're a knitter, knit ribbed cuffs instead of crocheting them. For the shawl portion, you could substitute nearly any bulky, drapey yarn—but be sure to check your gauge!

The Big Doily Wrap

Adapted from a vintage doily, this wrap is very *ooh-la-la*. The alpaca is very soft and not a bit itchy. The Aurora is a bit itchy, but it looks great and the itchy parts are well away from the neck area. But how do you *wear* a *doily*? Easy! Fold it in half and loop one end through a hole—or pin it up with part or all of the elegant three-in-one shell pin (I give you instructions for that, too).

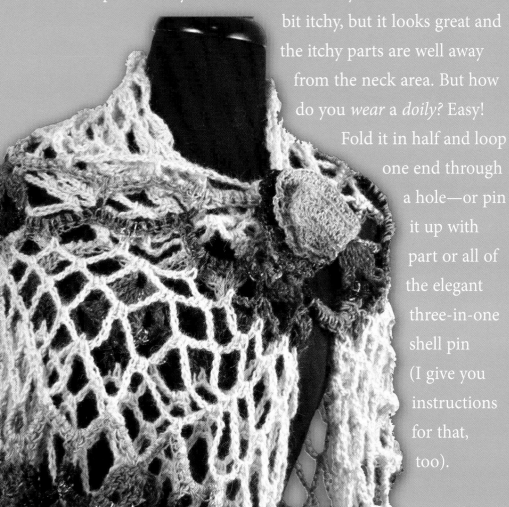

You'll look for occasions you can dress up in your Big Doily Wrap.

Skill level:
111

Yarn:
Frog Tree (100% alpaca, 50 g, 130 yd.): 2 balls color 005 (A); Noro Aurora (55% wool, 20% kid mohair, 20% silk, 5% polyester, 40 g, 104 m), 3 balls color 1 (B)

Crochet hook:
K (6.5mm)

Notions:
Tapestry needle
Pin backs

Finished size:
48 inches in diameter (folded in half, it will drape about 2 feet down from the shoulder)

Gauge:
Varies, but keep your stitches loose!

See? It really is a big doily.

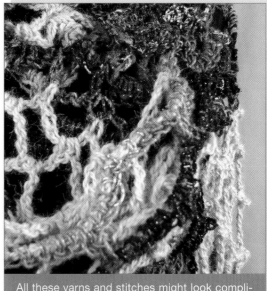

All these yarns and stitches might look complicated, but you can do it!

Two notes before you begin: you can substitute nearly any lightweight fiber for the Frog Tree, but work up a swatch to be sure you can get an airy effect with it. And you work this doily from front side only; do not turn it. Now let's go!

With A, ch 6. Join with a sl st to first ch to form a circle.

R1: Ch 9 (counts as 1 tr plus 1 ch-5). *Work 1 tr, ch 5, rep from * 6 times. Join with sl st to top of ch-4 (8 tr).

R2: Ch 1. In ch-5 spaces, work (3 sc, ch 3, 3 sc). Join with sl st in first ch.

R3: Sl st across top of sc to ch-3 loop, ch 4 (counts as first tr). Work cl, ch 5, work second cl in same space. *Ch 7; in next ch-3 loop, work (1 cl, ch 5, 1 cl). Rep from * around. Ch 7. Join with sl st in top of first cl (8 sets of 2 cl).

Remember the cluster (cl) stitch from Chapter 2? If not, here's a cheat sheet: work 3 tr, leaving last loop of each st on hook. Yo and pull through all loops on hook.

1 **R4:** Sl st to second ch of ch-5 loop. *Sc in ch-5 loop. Ch 7. In next ch-7 loop work (sc, ch 7, sc). Rep from * around, ending with (ch 3, tr) into first sc.

Ending with (ch 3, tr) into first sc brings the yarn to the center of the loop, ready to start the next round.

Here's the pattern: each row increases by 1 chain, which conveniently corresponds to the row number (5 chains in row 5, 6 chains in row 6, etc.). Put a stitch marker in the first single crochet of the round so you know when you're done. Move the marker as you start each new row.

Chain 3, triple crochet brings you right round.

R5: 2 sc over tr. *Ch 5, 2 sc in next loop. Rep from * around, ending with ch 1, tr in first sc.

R6: 2 sc over tr. *Ch 6, 2 sc in next loop. Rep from * around, ending with ch 2, tr in first sc.

R7: 2 sc over tr. *Ch 7, 2 sc in next loop. Rep from * around, ending with ch 3, tr in first sc.

R8: 2 sc over tr. *Ch 8, 2 sc in next loop. Rep from * around, ending with ch 3, dtr in first sc.

R9: 1 sc over tr. *Ch 9, 1 sc in next loop. Rep from * around, ending with ch 9, sl st in first sc. Cut yarn.

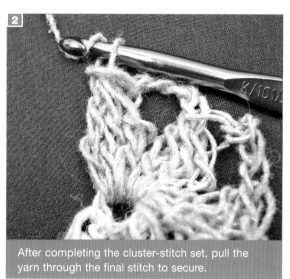

After completing the cluster-stitch set, pull the yarn through the final stitch to secure.

Note that in rows 9 and 19, you work only 1 sc, rather than 2, in each loop.

R10: Join B with sl st in any loop, ch 1, and work (5 sc, ch 3, 5 sc) in each loop, join in first sc. Cut yarn.

2 **R11:** Rejoin B with sl st in any ch-3 loop. *In same space: ch 4 (counts as first tr), work cl, ch 4, cl, ch 4, cl. Pull loop through final st again to secure, and cut yarn.

Sk 2 ch-3 spaces. Join yarn in next ch-3 loop, and repeat from * around (8 groups of 3 cl).

R12: Attach B with sl st in first ch-3 loop after any cl group; sc in same space *ch 8, sc in next ch-3 loop, ch 7, 5 sc in next loop between cl sts, ch 3, 5 sc in next loop between cl sts, ch 7, sc in next ch-3 loop, repeat from * around, ending ch 7, join with sl st in first sc.

R13: *In next ch-8 loop (5 sc, ch 3, 5 sc); in next ch-7 loop (4 sc, ch 3, 4 sc); ch 5; in next ch-3 loop (1 sc, ch 3, 1 sc); ch 5; in next ch-7 loop (4 sc, ch 3, 4 sc), rep from * around. Join with sl st to first sc. Cut yarn.

 At this point, you will have about a thousand dangling ends. Take a few minutes now to weave them in and you will be less annoyed—and when you're done the wrap, you'll have half as many ends to weave in.

R14: Join A with sl st in ch-3 loop above any cl st group, sc in same space *ch 5, sc in next ch-5 loop; ch 5; sc in next ch-3 loop; (ch 7, sc in next ch-3 loop) twice; ch 5; sc in next ch-5 loop; ch 5; sc in ch-3 loop; ; rep from * around, to sc in last ch-5; ch 1, tr in first sc.

R15: 2 sc over tr. *Ch 6, 2 sc in next loop. Rep from * around, ending with ch 2, tr in first sc.

R16: 2 sc over tr. *Ch 7, 2 sc in next loop. Rep from * around, ending with ch-3, tr in first sc.

R17: 2 sc over tr. *Ch 8, 2 sc in next loop. Rep from * around, ending with ch 3, dtr in first sc.

R18: 2 sc over tr. *Ch 9, 2 sc in next loop. Rep from * around, ending with ch 4, dtr in first sc.

R19: 1 sc over tr. *Ch 9, 1 sc in next loop. Rep from * around, ending with ch 9, join with sl st in first sc. Cut yarn.

R20: Join B in any loop, ch 1, and work (5 sc, ch 3, 5 sc) in each loop, join with sl st in first sc.

R21: Rejoin B in any ch-3 loop. *In same space ch 4 (counts as first tr), work cl, ch 4, cl, ch 4, cl; pull loop through final st again to secure, and cut yarn. Sk 2 ch-3 spaces. Join yarn in next ch-3 loop, and repeat from * around (16 groups of 3 cl).

R22: Attach B in first ch-3 loop after any cl st group; sc in same space. *Ch 8, sc in next ch-3 loop, ch 7, 5 sc in next loop between cl sts, ch 3, 5 sc in next loop between cl sts, ch 7, sc in next ch-3 loop, repeat from * around, join with sl st in first sc.

R23: *In next ch-8 loop (5 sc, ch 3, 5 sc); in next ch-7 loop (4 sc, ch 3, 4 sc); ch 5; in next ch-3 loop (1 sc, ch 3, 1 sc); ch 5; in next ch-7 loop (4 sc, ch 3, 4 sc), rep from * around. Join with sl st to first sc. Cut yarn.

Weave in the many, many ends.

 When using a variegated yarn such as the Noro Aurora in this project, wind the yarn off the ball or skein until you get to the color you want. Break the yarn, and you're ready to go.

Shell pins:

To make three pins: Wind off 3 colors from the multi-colored ball of Aurora. I used a length of purple for the small one, green for the medium, and black for the large. Make a small shell by working through row 5, a medium shell by working through row 6, and a big shell by working through row 7. You'll end up with three sizes of shells.

3 With chosen color from Aurora, ch 4.

R1: In fourth ch from hook, work 6 dc (7 dc, including tch). Turn.

R2: Ch 3. Sk first st. Working in back loop only, dc in next 2 sts, 3 dc in next st, dc in next 2 sts and in tch (9 dc, including tch). Turn.

R3: Ch 3. Sk first st. Working in back loop only, dc in next 3 sts, 3 dc in next st, dc in next 3 sts and in tch (11 dc, including tch). Turn.

R4: Ch 3. Sk first st. Working in back loop only, dc in next 4 sts, 3 dc in next st, dc in next 4 sts and in tch (13 dc, including tch). Turn.

R5: Ch 3. Sk first st. Working in back loop only, dc in next 6 sts, 3 dc in next st, dc in next 5 sts and in tch (15 dc, including tch). Turn.

R6: Ch 3. Sk first st. Working in back loop only, dc in next 7 sts, 3 dc in next st, dc in next 6 sts and in tch (17 dc, including tch). Turn.

R7: Ch 3. Sk first st. Working in back loop only, dc in next 7 sts, 3 dc in next st, dc in next 7 sts and in tch (19 dc, including tch).

Break off yarn. Weave in ends.

4 Sew pin to back of shell. If you will wear all 3 together, be sure not to overlap the pins.

Make It Your Own

Try different colors and textures here. But no matter what yarn you use, be sure to keep your stitches loose.

Make three sizes of shells for the wrap-securing pin or just one. The choice is yours.

Sew the pin to the back of the shell.

If you're not crazy about using the pins to secure the wrap, you can simply pull one end through a hole.

Short skirts are always hip (if you're shy about your gams, don't worry—I offer easy increasing tips here, too). Knit Picks Twist yarn is a fabulous blend of earthy and pastels that works up into a lovely tweed fabric. It looks like fine silk suiting, but with a bit of bling. Worked in this yarn, the shell stitch is very subtle (see note on yarn substitutions following the materials list), so the touch of contrasting color highlights the lovely scallops. Working the skirt side to side, rather than waistband to hem, allows for sitting-down stretch and avoids the sagging-hem issue.

A crochet skirt? Sure! Try this Maximal Skirt on for size.

Maximal Skirt

If you substitute yarns, work up a swatch before you commit to a large amount of yarn. And be sure it gives you the coverage and aesthetic appeal you want. A heavier yarn will be warmer, but may give the impression that you whacked off a swath of afghan to wear around your waist.

You can easily alter the size of this skirt. Make it longer by increasing the starting chain by 6 chains for every 1¼ inches desired (1 shell equals 1¼ inches). Make it wider by crocheting more rows.

It's the nature of crochet to be a bit peek-a-boo. This skirt is very wearable over leggings or tights. You can also wear a short slip under it.

With yarn A and size H hook, ch 44.

R1: In fifth ch from hook, work 4 dc in ch, *sk 2 ch, sc in next ch, sk 2 ch, 5 dc in next ch. Rep from *, ending with sc (7 shells). Turn.

R2: Ch 2. 2 dc in sc. *In center dc of shell (sk 2 dcs) sc; 5 dc in sc, rep from * across, ending with 3 dc in tch (6 full shells; 2 half shells). Turn.

R3: Ch 1. *5 dc in sc; in center dc of shell, sc; rep from *, ending with sc in tch (7 shells). Turn.

Repeat rows 2 and 3 until piece is 42 inches long (or long enough to wrap 2 inches below your waist with 8-inch overlap).

Join B. Work 2 rows shell stitch. Cut yarn.

Waistband:

To determine the top of the skirt, wrap the skirt left side first, then right side over, with scalloped edge on the outside.

Be sure to switch to the smaller hook here—this will draw in the waist a bit.

With yarn B and hook G, work shell stitch in row 2 evenly across the top.

Work 3 more rows in shell stitch pattern.

Skill level:
/ / /

Yarn:
Knit Picks Twist (30% cotton, 30% viscose, 20% acrylic, 20% nylon, 50 g, 99 yd.), 5 balls each Parrot 14439-7 (A), 1 ball Beach Ball 14439-11 (B)

Crochet hook:
H (5mm),
G (4.25mm)

Notions:
Tapestry needle
Sewing needle
Thread
Bit of fabric (about 2 inches square)
¾-inch button (or size to fit between hole in shell stitch)
Hook and eye closure

Finished size:
14 inches long by 41 inches around (to fit 33-inch waist, with 8-inch overlap)

Gauge:
Shell stitch: 2½ shells and 8 rows equals 4 inches

Sew the hook to the inner edge.

Stabilize button by sewing through a scrap of fabric on the back.

Fasten the button, and you're ready to go!

Pull end through final stitch. Cut yarn. Weave in ends.

1. Try on skirt to determine hook placement. Mark with a pin. Sew the hook to the inner edge, about $\frac{1}{4}$ inch down from the top edge and 1 inch from the side edge. Sew the eye at the corresponding point inside the skirt.

2. 3. Try on skirt to determine button place. Mark with a pin, and sew on button, using a bit of fabric as a backing to hold button securely. Use the space between the shell as the buttonhole.

Wrap it on, and hit the town!

Make It Your Own

You can work the waistband in a contrast color for a little more pop. Or experiment with different yarns—look for a yarn with a bit of elasticity.

Keep Cozy

In This Chapter

Have some fun with
Never-Too Scarves

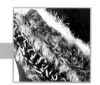

Make him something with
His Scarf

Cold wrists? Warm them up with
Wrist Warmers

Warm your neck (and your heart) with
the Rippled Cowl

Top it off with a Basic Hat

This medley of winter wearables offers different kinds of comforts—the ultra-skinny Never-Too Scarves heat up an outfit, and His Scarf is a truly cozy neck warmer. The Wrist Warmers work inside and out, as does the Rippled Cowl. And the Basic Hat is a blank slate waiting for your personal touch. Although the projects in this chapter use a variety of stitch techniques, they're all very portable, so you can work on them in meetings and at long stoplights. Have fun!

"You can never be too rich or too thin"—indeed, as these slender, sumptuous scarves prove. And I'll go ahead and apologize now, because I know what's going to happen: you're going to make one and say, "Hey, that was fast! And it looks fabulous! I wonder what it would look like in, say, red and silver or in Mardi Gras colors …" and you'll be off to your LYS to cook up some more combinations. Before long, you'll just bring your folding chair right to the shop and crochet straight off the shelves because you won't be able to stop. Enjoy!

A medley of skinny scarves. Bottom left to top right: the Noel, Cruella De Ville, Thin Mint, Blue Suede, and Frost Scarves.

Never-Too Scarves

All these scarves follow the same basic pattern but use the different colors noted in each scarf's section. Any alterations are noted under the scarf's materials list.

Holding all the yarns together, chain as many chains as you want. I averaged 100 to 150 chains long.

R1: Dc in fourth ch and in every ch across.

R2: There is no row 2! Cut the yarn and pull through the final stitch. Weave in ends.

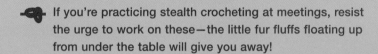 If you're practicing stealth crocheting at meetings, resist the urge to work on these—the little fur fluffs floating up from under the table will give you away!

Skill level:
/ / /

Yarn:
See individual scarf sections

Crochet hook:
P (11.5mm),
Q (15mm)

Notions:
Tapestry needle

Finished size:
Varies

Gauge:
Varies

Thin Mint Scarf

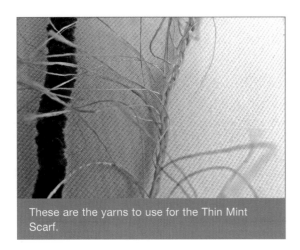

These are the yarns to use for the Thin Mint Scarf.

Yarn:

Lion Suede (100% polyester, 3 oz., 122 yd.), 1 ball Coffee 126 (A); Lion Fun Fur (100% polyester, 50 g, 60 yd.), 1 ball Lime 320-158

Crochet hook:

P (11.5mm)

Blue Suede Scarf

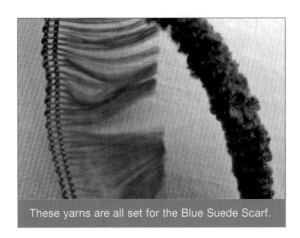

These yarns are all set for the Blue Suede Scarf.

Yarn:

Lion Suede (100% polyester, 3 oz., 122 yd.), 1 ball Teal 178 (A); Bernat Boa (100% polyester, 50 g, 71 yd.), 1 ball Peacock 81205

Crochet hook:

P (11.5mm)

Cruella De Ville Scarf

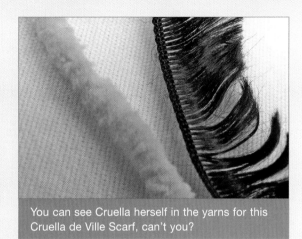

You can see Cruella herself in the yarns for this Cruella de Ville Scarf, can't you?

Noel Scarf

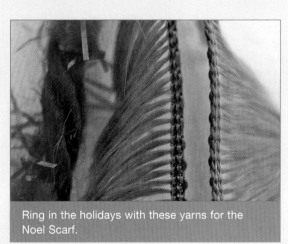

Ring in the holidays with these yarns for the Noel Scarf.

Yarn:

Lion Suede (100% polyester, 3 oz., 122 yd.), 1 ball Ecru 210-098; Bernat Boa (100% polyester, 50 g, 71 yd.), 1 ball Raven 81040

Crochet hook:

P (11.5mm)

Yarn:

Bernat Ping Pong (73% acrylic, 27% nylon, 50 g, 58 yd.), 1 ball Radiant Red 51430 (A); Bernat Boa (100% polyester, 50 g, 71 yd.), 2 balls Mallard 81236 (B)

Crochet hook:

P (11.5mm)

Use 1 strand of A and 2 strands of B. Work only the chain. Do not make the row of double crochet.

If you're tempted to use one ball of Boa and pull the yarn from both ends to make two strands, don't do it! The ensuing tangle will make the project most unfun.

Frost Scarf

You'll want to warm up with these yarns for the Frost Scarf.

Use a size Q hook to handle these 5 strands. Chain *very loosely* to the desired length and then end. No double crochet here.

Yarn:

Bernat Boa (100% polyester, 50 g, 71 yd.), 1 ball Dove 81005; Lion Festive Fur (100% polyester, 50 g, 60 yd.), 1 ball each White 570-100 and Silver 570-150; Patons ChaCha (100% nylon, 50 g, 77 yd.), 1 ball Waltz 02011; Patons Brilliant (69% acrylic, 19% nylon, 12% polyester, 50 g, 166 yd.), 1 ball White Twinkle 3005

Crochet hook:

Q (15mm)

Make It Your Own

You can make a short, fat scarf if you want. Just make fewer starting chains and double crochet more rows. What else can you think of to do with these easily adjusted scarves?

His Scarf

They can be so fussy—nothing too itchy, too colorful, too long, too short, too whatever. Men! But here's a scarf he'll love. The soy blended with the wool in this yarn keeps it soft—no itch here. The tweedy texture—made by double-crocheting in the single crochets and single crocheting in the double crochets—is tailored enough to go with a top coat, but the earthy colors make it good with a leather or denim jacket. Dare him to find something to fuss about! (Oh, and it's super easy! But don't tell him that!)

Presenting a scarf he'll love: His Scarf.

Skill level:
1

Yarn:
Patons SWS (70% wool, 30% soy, 80 g, 110 yd.), 3 balls Natural Navy 70130

Crochet hook:
I (5.5mm)

Notions:
Tapestry needle

Finished size:
6½ inches wide by 52 inches long

Gauge:
In pattern stitch: 12½ stitches and 12 rows equals 4 inches

Here's the pattern—not too frilly, just manly enough.

A couple of notes on yarn: When using variegated yarn, to match up stripes when you start a new ball, wind off the yarn until you get to the same color. Tie on, and go! And be wary of substituting yarns. This yarn was carefully researched with several menfolk. I can't guarantee they'll like anything else!

Ch 23.

R1: In third ch from hook, dc, *sc in next ch, dc in next, rep from * to end.

R2: Ch 3, *sc in dc, dc in sc, rep from *, end dc in final sc.

R3: Ch 2, *dc in sc, sc in dc, rep from * end sc in final dc.

If you lose count, just look at the next stitch. If it's a single crochet, double crochet into it; if it's a double crochet, single crochet into it.

Repeat rows 2 and 3 for pattern to desired length.

Cut yarn. Weave in ends.

Make It Your Own

Make it longer, shorter, fatter, or skinnier—but for goodness sake, no frilly edging!

Wrist Warmers

The office is freezing, but you have to use your computer. Sure, you could cut the fingers off some gloves, but for a classier option, slip on these wrist warmers. The sumptuous wool/silk blend crochets up nicely—and you can whip them up during a couple office meetings.

These Wrist Warmers will soon become your favorite office accessory.

Skill level:
/ / /

Yarn:
Sundara yarn aran silky merino (50% silk, 50% merino wool, 100 g, 200 yd.), 1 ball Berries and Cream (This yarn is hand-dyed in small batches, so your color will be unique.)

Crochet hook:
G (4.25mm) or size needed to obtain gauge

Notions:
Tapestry needle

Finished size:
6½ inches wide by 6½ inches long

Gauge:
Single crochet 16½ stitches and 16 rows equals 4 inches

Slip stitch the first 5 stitches together.

This wrist warmer is sized to fit a palm 6½ inches in circumference. As you near the end, wrap the piece around your hand to fit it and adjust as necessary. You want it a bit stretchy so it doesn't bind, but not so loose that it flops around.

Ch 26.

R1: Sc in second ch and in every ch across (25 sts). Ch 1, turn.

R2–35: Working in back loop only, sc across (25 sts). Ch 1, Turn.

When done, do not cut yarn.

1 To join, holding the 2 long sides together, sl st the first 5 sts tog, through 1 loop only from each side. Cut yarn.

Reattach yarn at wrist end. Sl st 12 stitches together. Try on wrist warmer to check comfort around thumb, and add or subtract slip stitches to fit. Cut yarn.

Weave ends in. Turn seam to inside.

Edging:

2 **R1:** At wrist side, attach yarn with sl st. Sc in same st as sl st and then sc around in end of each row. Join to first sc with sl st.

3 **R2:** Sc in same stitch as sl st. *Sk 2 sc, 5 dc in next sc, sk 2 sc, sc in next sc. Rep from * around, ending with sc in final st.

If you've resized the wrist warmer, you might not end at the same place. Add or subtract a shell as needed. Close a gap of 1 or 2 sc by using the tail to sew the gap closed.

Cut yarn. Weave tails inside wrist warmer.

Attach yarn at the wrist with a slip stitch.

Make It Your Own

To make a longer wrist warmer, add more chains to the foundation row. To fit a smaller hand, crochet fewer rows; to fit a larger hand, crochet more rows.

Work shell stitch around the wrist edge.

Rippled Cowl

Sometimes you need something more than a turtle-neck but less than a scarf. Here it is: a cozy neck warmer. The cotton yarn adds color, and the mohair gives it a fuzzy halo. If you're feeling flush, make this in cashmere. The simple peek-a-boo chevron pattern is worked in the round.

Skill level:
///

Yarn:
Rowan Kidsilk Haze (70% super kid mohair, 30% silk, 25 g, 229 yd.), 1 balls Splendour 579; Lana Grosa Toccata Print (100% mako cotton, 50 g, 110 m), 2 balls 337

Crochet hook:
H (5mm)

Notions:
Tapestry needle
Stitch marker

Finished size:
20 inches circumference by 9 inches tall

Gauge:
Double crochet 12 stitches and 7 rows equals 4 inches

This Rippled Cowl will warm you right up.

The pattern of this cowl is so pretty.

Work 2 double crochets together over 2 chains.

Itchy, itchy, itchy! To test a yarn for itch, hold the ball against your neck for a few moments. If you feel a bit of an itch, you'll feel a *big* itch when you're wearing the cowl.

Make It Your Own

If you're not feeling flush enough for cashmere, a washable wool would be a very nice choice.

The pattern used for this cowl is essentially the same from row to row, but the beginning and end of the first 5 rounds differ, so pay attention!

With A and B held together, ch 90. Join to first ch with sl st, being careful not to twist chain.

1 **R1:** Ch 3 (counts as 1 dc). Work 2 dc, *dc 2 tog, skipping 2 chains between dc, 3 dcs, ch 2, 3 dc. Rep from * to end. Ch 2. Join to top of starting ch-3. Place marker at beginning of round, and move at the end of each round. Do not turn.

To work 2 dc together with 2 chains in between, yarn over, insert the hook in the stitch and pull up. Yarn over and pull through 2 loops on hook. Yarn over and insert hook in next designated stitch. Pull up loop and pull through 2 loops on hook. Yarn over and pull through all 3 loops on hook.

R2: Ch 3. *2 dcs, dc 2 tog, skipping (dc 2 tog) between dcs, 2 dc, in ch-2 space work (dc, ch 2, dc), rep from * around. Join to top of starting ch-3 with sl st.

R3: Chain 3. 1 dc *dc 2 tog, skipping (dc 2 tog) between dcs, 2 dc, in ch-2 space work (dc, ch 2, dc), 2 dcs, rep from * around. Dc in final dc. Join to top of starting ch-3 with sl st.

R4: Chain 2. Sk (dc 2 tog), 3 dc *in ch-2 space, work (dc, ch 2, dc), 2 dcs, dc 2 tog, skipping (dc 2 tog) between dcs, 2 dc, rep from * around. Join to top of starting ch-3 with sl st.

R5–16: Ch 3. Sk 1 dc, 3 dc *in ch-2 space, work (dc, ch 2, dc), 2 dcs, dc 2 tog, skipping (dc 2 tog) between dcs, 2 dc, rep from * around. Skip last dc. Join to top of starting ch-3 with sl st.

Cut yarn. Weave in ends.

A Basic Hat

Sometimes you just need something like this hat to keep your head warm. You can make just the basic hat in a fun yarn like Kureyon that does the color-changing magic for you, or you can jazz it up with embellishments: a flower or an edging. You can make a bigger hat by using a fatter yarn or a smaller hat by using a thinner yarn (with the correct corresponding hook, of course!). Or alter the increase rows—fewer for a smaller hat, more for a larger hat. Make the hat longer to create a fold-up brim. Have at it—it's your hat!

This hat will keep your noggin warm—and looking good!

Skill level:
/ / /

Yarn:
Noro Kureyon (100% wool, 50 g, 100 m), 1 ball color 58

Crochet hook:
H (5.0mm)

Notions:
Tapestry needle

Finished size:
19 inches in circumference, 7 inches deep

Gauge:
Single crochet 16 stitches and 16 rows equals 4 inches

Love that Noro color!

Ch 3. Join with sl st to form ring.

R1: In ring, work 6 sc. Do not join.

R2: Work 2 sc in each sc (12 sc).

R3: *Sc in 1 sc, 2 sc in next sc. Rep from * around (18 sc).

R4: *Sc in each of 2 sc, 2 sc in next sc. Rep from * around (24 sc).

R5: *Sc in each of 3 sc, 2 sc in next sc. Rep from * around (30 sc).

R6: *Sc in each of 4 sc, 2 sc in next sc. Rep from * around (36 sc).

R7: *Sc in each of 5 sc, 2 sc in next sc. Rep from * around (42 sc).

R8: *Sc in each of 6 sc, 2 sc in next sc. Rep from * around (48 sc).

R9: *Sc in each of 7 sc, 2 sc in next sc. Rep from * around (54 sc).

R10: *Sc in each of 8 sc, 2 sc in next sc. Rep from * around (60 sc).

R11: *Sc in each of 9 sc, 2 sc in next sc. Rep from * around (66 sc).

R12: *Sc in each of 10 sc, 2 sc in next sc. Rep from * around (72 sc).

R13: *Sc in each of 11 sc, 2 sc in next sc. Rep from * around (78 sc).

R14–30: Work even in sc.

Cut yarn. Weave in ends.

Make It Your Own

Add a flower. Add an edging. Add some surface crochet. This is a basic hat that's just waiting for you to embellish it!

Kids of All Ages

In This Part

Babies just wanna have fun. They don't want to wriggle around in a lacy thing; they want to roll around on a lush playmat in a stylish kimono. When you give these giggly gifts at a baby shower, the mama will love you all the more! And for mama herself, how about the kickin' sleep goggles? Dad might like the ice cream cozy with a lanyard, for those late-night feedings when one hand has to hold the baby's bottle. For the kids in between, you'll find a bunch of fun toys in this part, too.

But you don't have to hold to age restrictions: we actually had to wrassle Marley (see Chapter 10) off the hand of a 50-year-old. These projects are pure fun—have fun making them!

Oh, Baby!

In This Chapter

Dress up your favorite little one with a
Kimono and Kap

Keep it clean with the
Mess Blocker Washcloth

Cuddle up little one with the
Point-Counterpoint Blanket

Have some fun with the
Nice Cubes

Baby (and adults) will love the
Love That Bib!

When I think of babies, I think of bright colors—with a dash of drool. The baby-related projects in this chapter are easy-care, slightly unconventional patterns for cool babies. And as always, there's room for your own personal touch. Have fun!

Why should grown-ups have all the fun with the luxe yarns? This baby coat is simply elegant, worked up in merino tape by the oh-so-luxe folks at Colinette. When baby outgrows it—as babies are wont to do—it will make a fine teddy bear jacket. Oh, and did I mention how fast it is to work up? It's fast. You work the kimono almost in one piece—from the bottom of the back to the front, adding the sleeves as you go, down the front. And you'll have plenty of yarn left to work up the quick hat, which shapes around the baby's head in the center, leaving two cute points.

You'll get many compliments when you dress up the little one in this fun Kimono and Kap.

This yarn looks like an Impressionist painting.

Baby Kimono and Kap

Kimono

Ch 21.

R1: Sc in second ch from hook and across (20 sts). Turn.

R2–10: Ch 2, dc across (do not work sc in tch) (20 sts). Turn.

R11 (begin sleeve): Ch 9. In second ch from hook, work sc, then work sc in remaining chains and across back (28 sts).
Ch 9 (for second sleeve). Turn.

Note that whenever you add a section with chains, 1 row is worked in single crochet.

R12: Sc in second ch from hook and across remaining chains, back, and first sleeve (36 sts). Turn.

R13–17: Ch 2. Dc across (36 sts).

R18 (begin right front and sleeve, and shape neck): Ch 2. Dc in 14 sts. Turn.

R19: Ch 2. Dc across (14 sts).

R20: Ch 2. Dc across. Do not turn.

R21 (start first front section): Ch 7. Turn. Sc in second ch from hook and across (20 sts).
R22–23: Ch 2, dc across. Turn.

R24: Ch 1, *sc* across.

R25 (end sleeve 1): Ch 2. Dc in 12 sts.

R26–33: Ch 2. Dc across (12 sts). Turn.
R34: Ch 1. Sc across. End.

Skill level:
111

Yarn:
Colinette Taliatelli (90% merino wool, 10% nylon, 100 g, 145 m), 2 skeins Gauguin 100

Crochet hook:
M (9mm)

Notions:
Tapestry needle
2 (14-inch) lengths
¼-inch-wide ribbon

Finished size:
9½ inches wide by 10½ inches long (to fit 6 months)

Gauge:
Double crochet 9½ stitches and 5 rows equals 4 inches

If you can't splurge for 2 skeins of yarn, you can work the kimono with 1 skein if you shorten the coat by 1 double crochet row on both the back and the front. You won't have leftovers for the hat, though.

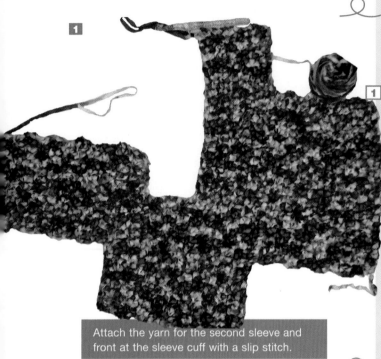

Attach the yarn for the second sleeve and front at the sleeve cuff with a slip stitch.

Before you go about adding the second front, take a moment to marvel that you looped up that curious shape out of a single strand of yarn. Yay! You're a marvel!

1 Rejoin yarn at cuff of second sleeve.

R1: Join yarn with sl st. Ch 2. Dc in 14 sts.

R2: Ch 2. Dc across.

R3: Ch 2. Dc across. Do not turn.

R4 (start second front): Ch 7. Turn. Work sc in second ch from hook and across chains and sleeve (20 sc).

R5–7: Ch 2. Dc across. Turn.

R8 (end second sleeve): Ch 2. Dc in 12 sts.

R9–16: Ch 2. Dc across. Turn.

R17: Ch 1. Sc across.

Cut yarn. Weave in ends.

Can't tell the inside from the outside? That's okay—it doesn't matter with this yarn. Just pick a side.

2 Fold kimono front over back and pin the
3 side seams. Sew the side seams and under sleeves with whip stitch, using doubled yarn.

Fold front over back …

… and sew the side seams.

4 Turn kimono right side out. Attach ribbon at corner of right front. Lap front over and attach second ribbon on left front where corner meets.

Kap

Ch 18.

R1: Sc in second chain from hook and across (17 sts). Turn.

R2–15: Ch 2. Dc across. Turn.

R16: Ch 1. Sc across.

Cut yarn. Weave in ends.

5 Fold rectangle in half widthwise, and sew up the side seams.

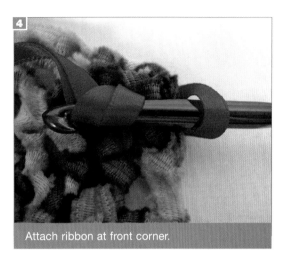

Attach ribbon at front corner.

Fold the hat in half and crochet the side seams together.

Make It Your Own

This is a simple enough design to adapt to different yarns, but as always, check your gauge! You could make tiny kimonos with fine yarn and use them as gift toppers, or make a batch in different colors and make a mobile. You can attach tassels to the top corners of the hat, too.

No mama can have too many wipes. This cheery, palm-size cloth looks like a trio of baby blocks. Plus, these all-cotton cloths pop right in the washer and dryer. Whip up a few and keep them on hand for baby presents.

No more messes with the Mess Blocker Washcloth.

Mess Blocker Washcloth

 You'll need to single crochet 2 together in this project. See Chapter 2 for refresher instructions if you need to.

With A, ch 16.

R1: In second chain from hook, work 1 sc and in every chain across (15 sc). Turn.

R2: Ch 1. Work first 2 sc tog, sc in each sc to end. Sc in top of tch (15 sc). Turn.

R3: Ch 1. Work even in sc across. Turn.

Repeat rows 2 and 3 to row 14 (you will end with row 2 repeat). On the last st of row 14, yo with color B and pull through final st. Cut A.

Attach color B with a yarn over.

 Joining a second yarn as a yarn over in the last stitch prevents the little color jog often caused when joining in a chain.

Skill level:

11

Yarn:

Lily Sugar 'n Cream (100% cotton, 2.5 oz., 120 yd.), 1 ball each Hot Pink 01740 (A), Hot Green 01712 (B), Hot Orange 01628 (C)

Crochet hook:

J (6mm)

Notions:

Tapestry needle

Finished size:

7 inches wide

Gauge:

Single crochet 13 stitches and 14 rows equals 4 inches

The second section slants in a different direction from A.

Attach C between A and B.

C slants back toward B.

With B, ch 2. Turn.

Pay attention! The B piece angles in a different direction from A.

5 **R1:** Work even in sc across A. Turn (15 sc).

R2: Ch 2. Sc in second ch from hook. Sc across to last 2 sc. Sc final 2 sc tog (15 sc). Turn.

R3: Ch 1. Work even in sc across (15 sc). Turn.

Repeat rows 2 and 3 to row 14 (you will end with a row 2 repeat). Cut B. End.

6 Attach C at center of block where A and B meet.

7 **R1:** Ch 1. Sc evenly 15 sc along edge of A. Turn (15 sc).

R2: Ch 1. Work first 2 sc tog, sc in each sc to end. Sc in top of tch (15 sc). Turn.

R3: Ch 1. Work even in sc across. Turn.

Repeat rows 2 and 3 to row 14. End, leaving a 12-inch tail.

8 Use the tail to sew up the seam between B and C.

Sew up the seam with the tail left over from C.

Make It Your Own

Color, color, color! Experiment with your favorite color combinations here. The illusion works best if A is a dark hue, B is light, and C is medium.

Point-Counterpoint Blanket

It's true that all your friends have babies at the same time. And because you're a crafter, they really expect something made lovingly by your hand. This blanket will rescue you! The intriguing point-to-point diagonal pattern keeps you entertained while you whip it up in no time. The yarn—dubbed, happily enough, Smile—spins out into the yummiest colors. The heavy weight lends itself to a play mat or stroller blanket.

Skill level:

///

Yarn:

Reynolds Smile (72% acrylic 28% wool, 100 g, 124 yd.), 5 balls Gold/ Fuchsia/Blue Multi 107

Crochet hook:

M (9mm)

Notions:

Tapestry needle

Finished size:

30 inches square

Gauge:

3 shells and 3 rows equals 4 inches (But it's a blanket! Gauge is not critical.)

All your expecting friends will expect the Point-Counterpoint Blanket for their shower gift!

The colors are so, so fun!

The very first shell.

The first 3 shells are slightly different from one another, so pay attention! By the third row, all will be clear and easy.

1 **R1** (first shell): Ch 5. In fifth ch from hook, work 3 dc. Turn.

2 **R2:** Make starting shell: ch 5. In fourth ch from hook, make 3 dc. Then sl st into next ch-3 space and make a regular shell (ch 3, work 3 dc). Turn.

3 **R3:** Make starting shell. Make shell in next 2 ch-3 spaces (3 shells total). Turn.

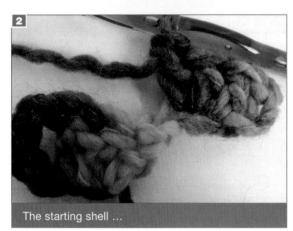

The starting shell ...

... and another shell. You've completed row 2.

The blanket after 3 rows.

4 **R4–24:** Make starting shell. Make shell in each ch-3 space across. Turn. You're not at the midpoint of your blanket.

When you need to attach new yarn, just tie the ends together with an overhand knot and trim the ends.

Where's the knot?! It's absorbed by the crochet stitches.

5   **R25:** *Begin decrease:* *Ch 1. Sk 1 st, sl st in next 2 sts and in ch-3 space *of last shell worked.* Make shell in this shell and in each ch-3 space across to last ch-3 space.

☞ Watch the beginning and ends of rows on the decrease to be sure you don't add a shell. You'll notice immediately if you do because it will stick out. If this happens, just pull out the shell.

To begin decrease, slip stitch across the first shell.

6   In last ch-3 space, sl st and turn; *do not work shell in final ch-3 space.* Turn. Rep Row 25 until 1 shell remains. Pull yarn through final stitch. Weave in ends.

Wait! Don't work that last shell. Just slip stitch into it.

Make It Your Own

This pattern works up beautifully in a lighter yarn with a smaller hook. You'll have to work more rows to reach 30 inches, of course.

These classic blocks feature a classic yarn: Red Heart acrylic. You could easily substitute organic cotton or anything else you like, but these blocks are going to experience a lot—gummy bites, strained carrots, dog slobber (hey, it happens!). The acrylic surface washes without trouble. The varied stitches give the baby some texture to play with and let you experiment with stitch combinations.

These soft, colorful Nice Cubes will keep baby entertained.

Nice Cubes

Note there are two yarns of each letter—one for each block—marked 1 and 2 accordingly. Of course it doesn't matter which color you use for which block—but knowing the colors I used will help you identify the pattern.

Why are there different numbers of rows for blocks that are the same size? Because different heights of stitches are used in the various patterns, so the rows are different heights. Patterns with shorter stitches have more rows than patterns with taller stitches.

Side 1

Cube side 1, worked in Crossed Single Crochet.

With A (Turqua or White), ch 12.

R1: Sc in second ch from hook and in each ch across (11 sts). Turn.

R2–8: Ch 1. Sc in first sc, *sk next sc, sc in skipped sc, rep from *.

Break yarn. Rejoin at bottom right and sc around 3 sides. End.

Skill level:
/ / /

Yarn:
Red Heart Super Saver (100% acrylic, 7 oz., 364 yd.), small amount each Turqua 0512 (A1), White 0311 (A2, E2), Bright Yellow 034 (B1), Black 0312 (B2, D2), Spring Green 0672 (C1), Hot Red 0390 (C2, F1, F2), Pumpkin 0254 (D), Blue 0886 (E)

Crochet hook:
I (5.5mm)

Notions:
Tapestry needle 3×3-inch foam blocks (available at upholstery or fabric shops)

Finished size:
3-inch cube

Gauge:
Varies

Cube side 2, worked in V stitch.

Side 3 of your cube, worked in spot stitch. This is where you add the bobbles.

Cube side 4, worked in single crochet ridge.

Side 2

1 With B (Bright Yellow or Black), ch 13.

R1: Sc in second ch from hook and in every ch to end (12 sc). Turn.

R2–10: Ch 1. *Sk 1 sc, 2 sc in next sc. Rep from * to end. Turn.

Side 3

2 With C (Spring Green or Hot Red), ch 13.

R1: Sc in second ch from hook and in every ch to end (12 sc). Turn.

R2: (wrong side) Ch 1, sk first sc, 1 sc into next sc. *In next st, work bobble: 5 dc tog in 1 st. (Yo, insert hook and draw up loop, yo and draw through 2 loops on hook) 5 times. Yo and draw through all 6 loops on hook. Sc 1 in each of next 3 sc, rep from *, ending 1 sc in last sc, 1 sc in tch.

R3–5: Ch 1, sk first sc, sc in each st to end.

R6–9: Repeat rows 2 through 5.

R10–13: Repeat rows 2 through 5. End.

Side 4

3 With D (Pumpkin or Black), ch 13.

R1: Sc in second chain and across (12 sc).

R2–11: Ch 1. Working in back loop only, sc in each sc across (12 sc). Turn.

Side 5

4 With E (blue or white), ch 13.

R1: Sk 2 ch (counts as one hdc), slip stitch in 3rd chain from hook. *hdc in next chain, slip stitch in next chain. Rep from * across (12 sts). Turn.

R2–10: Ch 2 (counts as 1 hdc). *Slip stitch into top of hdc, hdc into slip stitch. Rep from * across, ending with slip stitch in top of turning chains. Turn.

These blocks are perfect for testing out a pattern for a larger project. Think of them as a big swatch. Note that the 3-inch blocks aren't big enough for an official swatch— you can always get bigger foam cubes!

Cube side 5, worked in crunch stitch.

Side 6

5 With Red, ch 12.

R1: In second ch from hook, sc. *Dc in next ch, sc in next ch, rep from * across (11 sts). Turn.

R2–8: Ch 1 *sc in sc, dc in dc. Rep from * across (11 sts). Turn.

6 To assemble, sew 4 blocks together in a straight line.

Cube side 6, worked in crumpled griddle.

6 Sew together the black and white squares.

Sew on a red square.

Wrap the next square around the second side of the red block.

Insert foam block, and sew on the final side, the second red square.

7. Sew the fifth block to the bottom of the right-most square.

8. Wrap the next square around and sew on.

9. Continue until first 4 squares are attached to fifth square. Sew remaining open side. Turn right side out, insert the foam block, and sew on the final side.

Make It Your Own

Sugar'n Cream (used in the Mess Blocker Washcloth project earlier in this chapter) is another good choice for these blocks. Try a block with a different textured yarn on each side: eyelash yarn, boucle, silk, etc. Or do a block in all the same yarn. Or sew the blocks together—perhaps with a contrasting yarn—so the seam shows on the outside.

Love That Bib!

This bib reminds you that you love, love, love this sweet baby who is spitting strained peas out as fast as you can spoon them in. And if wailing wins the day, pop in the pacifier attached to the loop at the bottom of the bib. And, yes, those peas will wash right out of this baby-friendly cotton yarn.

Keep the Love That Bib! for you and your little one, or give it as a gift.

Skill level:
/ / /

Yarn:
Lily Sugar'n Cream (100% cotton, 2.5 oz., 120 yd.), 1 ball each Hot Blue 01742 (A), Warm Brown 01130 (B), Hot Pink 01740 (C), Pumpkin 01132 (D), Hot Green 01712 (E)

Crochet hook:
J (6mm)

Notions:
Tapestry needle
Hook-and-loop fastener dots
Pacifier

Finished size:
8 inches at widest point by 7½ inches from top of heart to point

Gauge:
Double crochet 12 stitches and 7 rows equals 4 inches

Join the pink yarn in the center single crochet of one side.

Attach to the square with a slip stitch.

Join the green yarn in the center space of the side adjacent to the side you just worked.

When alternating yarns every few rows, as you'll do in this project, you can simply carry the yarn up the side and don't have to mess with cutting it and later weaving in the ends. See Chapter 2 for a refresher.

With A, ch 16.

R1: Sc in second ch from hook and across (15 sc). Turn.

R2–3: Ch 2. Dc across. Turn.

R4–5: Join B and ch 1. Sc across. Turn.

R6–7: With A, ch 2. Dc across.

R8–9: With B, ch 1. Sc across.

R10–11: With A, ch 2. Dc across.

R12: With A, ch 1, sc across. Cut both yarns.

To make the upper right part of the heart, join C in center sc of one side.

R1: With C, ch 3 (counts as 1 dc). Work 7 dc in same sc (8 dc). Turn.

R2: Join D and ch 3. Work 1 dc in first dc. Work 2 dc in each of next 6 dc. Work 1 dc in final dc. Attach to bib with sl st (15 dc). Turn.

R3: Ch 3. Work 1 dc in first dc. *2 dc in next dc, 1 dc in next dc. Rep from * around, ending with 1 dc in final dc, 1 dc in top of tch (22 dc). End.

To make the upper right part of the heart, join E in center space of adjacent side.

R1: With E, ch 3. Work 7 dc in same sc (8 dc). Turn.

R2: Ch 3. Work 1 dc in first dc. Work 2 dc in each of next 6 dc. Work 1 dc in final dc. Attach to bib with sl st (15 dc). Turn.

R3: Join B. Ch 3. Work 1 dc in first dc. *2 dc in next dc, 1 dc in next dc rep from * around, ending with 1 dc in final dc, 1 dc in top of tch (22 dc). Cut yarn and pull through final stitch.

Weave in all ends.

Edging and ties:

4 With C, ch 40 (that's the tie base). Join tie to upper left of bib, 10 sts up from the square. Sc around edge of bib, stopping 10 sts up upper right side. Ch 41. Sc in second ch from hook and back along chains. Rejoin tie by sc in the next sc on edge of bib. Continue sc around top to first tie. Sc along chains of first tie. End.

Swirl and pacifier tie:

5
6 Using D, hold yarn behind center of bib and pull up loop. Ch st swirl shape onto bib. Cut yarn.

4 Join the tie to the edge of the upper-left part of the bib, 10 stitches up from the square.

5 Attach yarn for swirl, with yarn tail behind bib.

6 Reattach the yarn on the front side of the bib.

Rejoin the tie to the front of the bib with a slip stitch.

Attach hook and loop fastener dots. Use these to secure a pacifier to the bib.

Hold the yarn behind the bib and pull up a loop.

To make pacifier tie, reattach yarn on front of bib at last ch of swirl. Ch 15. Sc in second ch from hook and back down ch. Join to bib with sl st. End.

[7]

Weave in all ends, using tie end to reinforce tie attachment.

[8] Attach hook-and-loop dots at either end of underside of tie.

Make It Your Own

These bright colors are gender-neutral, but you might prefer a blue edging and tie—purple would be good, too!

We're Stuffed!

In This Chapter

All the wee ones in your life will want
Play Pals

Finger Puppets—for when you
need a little bit of fun

Practice your ventriloquism with the
Marley Hand Puppet

Showcase your favorite kid art with the
I Made This! Pillow

Stuffed with fiberfill, fingers, and hands, these projects are designed to spark creativity in minds young and old. After you work up these projects, you might be inspired to adapt some projects to your own child's artwork. Plus, these projects are a good way to get your children interested in crochet when they see how fun the results are!

With their asymmetrical limbs and watercolor wash yarn, these dolls look just like something a child would draw and color in. The head and body are stuffed, and the scribbly arms and legs are single crochet on a chain.

You'll have fun with Jack and Jane.

Play Pals

Skill level:

11

Yarn:

Reynolds Smile (72%
acrylic, 28% wool,
100 g, 124 yd.), 2 balls
color 101 (A); Lamb's
Pride Worsted (85%
Wool, 15% mohair,
4 oz., 190 yd.), 1 skein
Onyx 05 (B)

Crochet hook:

L (8mm), K (6.5mm)

Notions:

Tapestry needle
Fiberfill
Embroidery floss—red,
plus blue, brown, or
green if you embroider
eyes
Sewing needle
Thread
4 (1-inch) buttons for
eyes

Finished size:

Jane is about 14 inches
tall from head to bot-
tom of torso and 9
inches wide. Jack is 12
inches tall (he's a little
brother, after all) and 6
inches wide.

Gauge:

Single crochet 7
stitches and 10 rows
equals 4 inches

For both Jane and Jack, use the Lamb's Pride Worsted *doubled*. Or substitute Lamb's Pride Bulky and use a single strand.

Jane's body is a triangle. To make a triangle, increase in the first and last stitch of each row on the front. On the back row, single crochet without increasing. It's spelled out row by row in the pattern instructions.

Jane

Say hello to Jane.

Body (make 2):

With yarn A and size L hook, ch 2.

R1: In second chain from hook, 2 sc. Turn.

R2: Ch 1, work 2 sc. Turn.

R3: Ch 1, inc in each sc by working 2 sc in each sc (2 increases made; 4 sc). Turn.

To keep track of the right (increase) side, pin a stitch marker to the right side.

R4: Ch 1, sc in each sc across. Turn.

R5: Ch 1, inc in first sc, sc in each of next 2 sc. Inc in last sc (6 sc).

R6: Ch 1, sc in each sc across. Turn.

R7: Ch 1, inc in first sc, sc across to last sc; inc in last sc (8 sc). Turn.

R8: Ch 1, sc in each sc across. Turn.

R9: Ch 1, inc in first sc, sc across to last sc; inc in last sc (10 sc). Turn.

R10: Ch 1, sc in each sc across. Turn.

R11: Ch 1, inc in first sc, sc across to last sc; inc in last sc (12 sc). Turn.

R12: Ch 1, sc in each sc across. Turn.

R13: Ch 1, inc in first sc, sc across to last sc; inc in last sc (14 sc). Turn.

R14: Ch 1, sc in each sc across. Turn.

R15: Ch 1, inc in first sc, sc across to last sc; inc in last sc (16 sc). Turn.

R16: Ch 1, sc in each sc across. Turn.

R17: Ch 1, inc in first sc, sc across to last sc; inc in last sc (18 sc). Turn.

R18: Ch 1, sc in each sc across. Turn.

R19: Ch 1, inc in first sc, sc across to last sc; inc in last sc (20 sc). Turn.

R20: Ch 1, sc in each sc across. Turn.

R21: Ch 1, inc in first sc, sc across to last sc; inc in last sc (22 sc). Turn.

R22: Ch 1, sc in each sc across. Turn.

R23: Ch 1, inc in first sc, sc across to last sc; inc in last sc (24 sc). Turn.

R24: Ch 1, sc in each sc across. End.

Head (make 2):

Ch 2.

R1: In second ch from hook, 6 sc. Join with sl st to first sc. Do not turn.

R2: Ch 1. 2 sc in each sc around (12 sc).

R3: Ch 1. *1 sc in first sc, 2 sc in next sc, rep from * around (18 sc).

R4: Ch 1. *1 sc in each of next 2 sc, 2 sc in next sc, rep from * around (24 sc).

R5: Ch 1. *1 sc in each of next 3 sc, 2 sc in next sc, rep from * around (30 sc).

R6: Ch 1. *1 sc in each of next 4 sc, 2 sc in next sc, rep from * around (36 sc).

Cut off yarn. Weave in ends.

Hand 1:

R1: In second ch from hook, 6 sc. Join with sl st to first sc. Do not turn.

R2: Ch 1. 2 sc in each sc around (12 sc).

Hand 2:

R1: In second ch from hook, 6 sc. Join with sl st to first sc. Do not turn.

R2: Ch 1. 2 sc in each sc around (12 sc).

R3: Ch 1. *1 sc in first sc, 2 sc in next sc, rep from * around (18 sc).

Cut off yarn. Weave in ends.

Feet (make 2):

Ch 3.

1 **R1:** In second ch from hook, 1 sc. 3 sc in next ch. Working across back of chain, 2 sc in back of first chain. Join with sl st to first sc. Do not turn.

Single crochet along the back of the chain.

R2: Ch 1. 1 sc 1st sc and next 2 sc. 3 sc in next sc. 1 sc in each of next 2 sc. 2 sc in final sc. Join with sl st to first sc. End.

Weave in ends.

To make an oval, you single crochet across the front of the chain, increase in the end chain, and single crochet across the back of the chain.

To assemble Jane, weave in all ends on the face and body parts.

2. *Body:* Fold diamond in half to make 2 facing triangles. Using B doubled and size K hook, chain stitch 2 sides together, starting at the bottom left and working across the bottom.

Just before finishing, stuff with fiberfill and then finish chain stitching together.

3. *Head:* Sew on face: buttons for eyes and a backstitched mouth. For young children, embroider on the eyes instead of using buttons, which can be a choking hazard.

4. Hold the 2 head circles back to back. Chain stitch around the edge, stuffing just before closing. Sew the head to the body with a whipstitch.

Slip stitch the sides of the body together.

Back stitch Jane's mouth into a warm smile.

Sew the head to the body with a whipstitch.

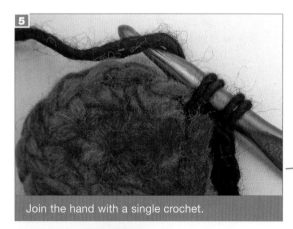

Join the hand with a single crochet.

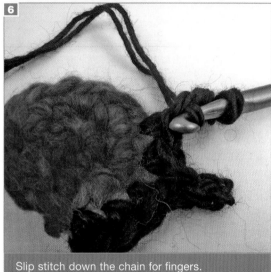

Slip stitch down the chain for fingers.

Pull the loop through to make Jane's hair.

5 6 *Arms:* Join B doubled at the desired arm location. Ch 14 to 18 (5 to 7 inches). Sc around one hand, making fingers as you go: ch 3 or 4, sl st in second ch and back to hand and continue sc to next finger location. Sc back up arm to body. Cut yarn. Weave in ends.

Be sure to vary the length of the arms, legs, and fingers as a child might in a drawing.

Repeat for second arm and hand.

Legs: Join B doubled at the desired arm location. Chain 22 to 25 (8 to 10 inches). Join foot by sc around edge of foot piece. Sc back up leg to body.

7 *Hair:* Cut about 12 (24-inch) lengths of yarn. Fold yarn in half and pull loops through loops on edge of head. Pull ends through loop.

Weave in ends.

Jack

Hi, Jack!

Body (make 2):

Ch 17.

R1: Sc in third ch from hook and across (15 sc). Turn.

R2–16: Ch 1. Sc across. Turn.

When piece is 6 inches long, end.

Hands (make 2):

R1: In second ch from hook, 6 sc. Join with sl st to first sc. Do not turn.

R2: Ch 1. 2 sc in each sc around (12 sc).

Foot 1:

Ch 4.

R1: Sc in second ch and next 2 ch (3 sc). Turn.

R2: Ch 1. Sc across. Turn.

R3: Ch 1. Sc across. End.

Foot 2:

Ch 5.

R1: Sc in second ch and next 2 ch (4 sc). Turn.

R2: Ch 1. Sc across. Turn.

Assemble Jack as you did Jane, but cut hair into 8-inch lengths.

Make It Your Own

These dolls would be fabulous in crayon colors. Use your own child's drawings to inspire your dolls.

This trio is up to no good—except having fun! Pop them on a child's finger and see what story unfolds. They're quick to crochet, so you could whip up a whole gang in no time.

A trio of unlikely buddies.

Finger Puppets

Legs

Legs—bet you can see where this little octopus puppet gets his name!

Skill level:

///

Yarn:

Red Heart Super Saver Multicolor (100% acrylic, 5 oz., 278 yd.), small amount Plum Pudding 285415

Crochet hook:

H (5mm)

Notions:

Tapestry needle
2 (⅜-inch) buttons for eyes
Sewing needle
Thread

Finished size:

3 inches tall by 5 inches around

Gauge:

Varies

Woolly

Like a sheep dog, Woolly is, well, woolly.

Skill level:

///

Yarn:

Tahki Donegal Tweed Homespun (100% wool, 100 g, 183 yd.), small amount 848 (or 867)

Crochet hook:

H (5mm)

Notions:

Tapestry needle
Black embroidery floss

Finished size:

3 inches tall by 5 inches around

Gauge:

Varies

Zippy

Zippy—he just looks fun (and a little mischievous).

Skill level:

///

Yarn:

Patons Classic Wool (100% wool, 3.5 oz., 223 yd.), small amount Regency 77731

Crochet hook:

H (5mm)

Notions:

Tapestry needle
2 (⅜-inch) buttons for eyes
1 heart button for mouth (optional)
Sewing needle
Thread

Finished size:

3 inches tall by 5 inches around

Gauge:

Varies

For Legs' legs, slip stitch down the chain.

Then single crochet in the next single crochet of the round.

Single crochet behind leg.

Legs

Ch 16. Join with sl st to first ch, being careful not to twist chain.

R1: Sc in each st (16 sc).

R2: *Sc in 2 sts (make leg), ch 9. Sc in second chain and next 7 ch. Rep from * sc in final sc. Then sc in next sc of round.

R3: Sc in each sc around, working behind legs.

R4–9: Sc in each sc around.

R10: Sc 2 tog around. Sc in final sc (8 sc).

R11: Sc around.

R12: Sc 2 tog around (4 sc).

Sew up hole at top, and weave in ends. Sew on eyes.

Woolly

Ch 15. Do not join.

R1: Ch 1. Sc across (15 sc).

R2: Ch 1. Sc in first sc. Work loop stitch (see Chapter 6) in next 13 sc. Sc in final sc. Turn.

R3: Ch 1. Sc in each sc. Turn.

R4: Work as row 2.

R5: Work as row 3.

R6: Work as row 2.

R7: Work as row 3.

R8: Work as row 2.

R9: Work as row 3.

R10: Ch 1. Sc in first sc. Loop stitch in next 2 sc. sc in next 3 sc (for face). Loop stitch in next 9 sc. Sc in final sc. Turn.

R11: Ch 1. Sc across.

R12: Ch 1. Sc in first sc. Loop stitch in next sc. Sc in next 5 sc. Loop stitch in next 7 sc.

Sc in final sc. Turn.

R13: Sc across. End.

 Embroider eyes and mouth in unlooped face area.

5 Turn inside out (so loop stitches are on the inside). Whipstitch the side seam, and turn right side out.

Fold Woolly in half, and with seam on right side, join yarn at top and work loop stitch across. End. Cut yarn.

For Woolly's ears, join yarn at top corner.

Ch 5. Sc in second ch from hook and next 3 ch. Join with sl st to corner. Weave in ends. Repeat for second corner.

Weave in ends.

Zippy

Ch 15. Join with sl st to first ch, being careful not to twist chain.

R1–12: Sc in each sc across. Do not cut yarn on last round.

Fold puppet. Sc across top. Cut yarn.

6 *Tail:*

Ch 18.

Work loop stitch across top of chain. Turn and work loop stitch across back of chain. End.

Attach tail with whipstitch to bottom of puppet and back of head. Cut loops and fluff out.

Sew on buttons for eyes and mouth.

Make It Your Own

These puppets take very little yarn to make. Dig into your stash and see what kind of puppet the yarn suggests. Green stuff would make a great alien. Blue might become an Abominable Snowman.

Sew on Woolly's eyes and mouth.

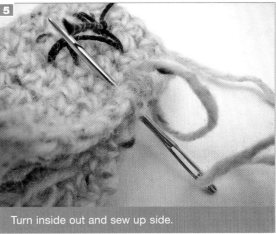

Turn inside out and sew up side.

Zippy is understandably proud of his tail.

I saw this yarn and had to have it! It's like a tie-dyed T-shirt turned into yarn. I challenged myself to find a project that would take exactly 1 ball of this yarn. (It almost worked—you need a second color for the inside of the mouth.)

Hey mon, it's Marley.

Marley Sock Puppet

Ch 30. Join with sl st to first ch, being careful not to twist.

R1: Sc in each ch around (30 sc). Do not join; work in a spiral.

R2–24: Sc in each sc around.

Bottom of mouth:

R25: Sc across 14 sc. Turn.

R26–35: Ch 1. Sc across. Turn.

R36: (Sc 2 tog) 7 times (7 sc). Turn.

R37: (Sc 2 tog) 3 times, sc in final sc (4 sc). Break off yarn.

Top of mouth:

(This piece is worked separately and then joined to the rest of the puppet.)

Ch 6.

R1: 2 sc in second ch from hook. 1 sc in next 3 ch, 2 sc in last ch (7 sc). Turn.

R2: Ch 1. 2 sc in first sc. 1 sc in next 2 sc, 2 sc in next sc, 1 sc in next 2 sc, 2 sc in last sc (10 sc). Turn.

R3: Ch 1. *1 sc in next sc, 2 sc in next sc, rep from * across (15 sc). Turn.

R4–12: Ch 1. Sc across. Turn.

Skill level:

1 1 1

Yarn:

Noro Kureyon (100% wool, 50 g, 100 m), 1 ball color 182 (A); Reynolds Lite-Lopi (100% wool, 50 g, 109 yd.), 1 ball color 0438

Crochet hook:

H

Notions:

Tapestry needle
2 (1-inch) buttons for eyes
Sewing needle
Thread

Finished size:

8 inches tall by 9 inches around

Gauge:

Single crochet 14 stitches and 16 rows equals 4 inches

Attach top of mouth at neck.

Single crochet across head again to work in the round.

Slip stitch the top of the head closed.

Head:

1 **R13:** Attach mouth top to neck: sc across back of neck (be sure the mouth curves downward at the lips). Sc across top of mouth. You will now work in the round.

2 Don't count rounds here. Just follow this pattern: sc 2 tog, sc 14, sc 2 tog, sc 13, sc 3 tog, sc 12, sc 3 tog, sc 11, sc 3 tog, sc 10, sc 3 tog, sc 9, sc 3 tog, sc 8, sc 3 tog, sc 7, sc 3 tog, sc 6, sc 3 tog, sc 5, sc 3 tog.

3 Hold front and back of head together and sl st 2 sides together. Cut yarn.

Weave in all ends.

Mouth:

(This piece is worked separately and then joined to the rest of the puppet.)

With B, ch 16.

R1: Sc in second ch from hook and across (15 sc). Turn.

R2: Ch 1. Inc in first sc, sc in next 13 sc, inc in last sc (17 sc). Turn.

R3: Ch 1, sc across. Turn.

R4: Ch 1. Inc in first sc, sc in next 17 sc, inc in last sc (19 sc). Turn.

R5: Ch 1, sc across. Turn.

R6–10: Ch 1, sc in back loop only. Turn.

Working ribbing through the center of the mouth, as in rows 6 through 10, allows it to expand for different size hands.

R11: Ch 1, sc in both loops across. Turn.

R12: Ch 1. Dec in first sc, sc in next 15 sc, dec in last sc (17 sc). Turn.

R13: Ch 1, sc across. Turn.

R14: Ch 1. Dec in first sc, sc in next 13 sc, dec in last sc (15 sc). Turn.

R15: Ch 1, sc across. End.

Weave in ends.

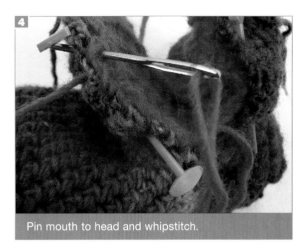

Pin mouth to head and whipstitch.

4. Turn Marley inside out and pin the mouth to the head. Whipstitch along the edges, and turn right side out.

Sew on buttons for eyes. If this puppet is intended for a child under 3, embroider eyes instead of using buttons.

Hair:

Cut 10 (24-inch) lengths of A. Fold in half and draw loop through top of head. Pull ends through. Marley's hair offers all sorts

5. of styling techniques: top knot, ponytail,
6. braid. Barrettes would be swell, too.

Try Marley's hair in a topknot …

Make It Your Own

Adapt this basic puppet to make a puppy, kitten, or your favorite critter. Just add ears, a tail, short hair—whatever makes it work.

… or a braid.

Run out of room on your fridge for your child's masterpieces? Take a favorite work and turn it into lasting art on a pillow. My daughter Kate drew this swell "Downward Facing Dog," and now she has a favorite pillow for naptime. Woof!

My daughter Kate's I Made This!
Pillow: Downward Facing Dog.

I Made This! Pillow

Skill level:
11

Yarn:
Patons Classic Wool
(100% wool, 3.5 oz.,
223 yd.), 1 ball Black
226 (A); Noro Cotton
Kureyon (70% cotton,
30% wool, 50 g, 100
m), 2 skeins color
14 (B)

Crochet hook:
H (5mm)

Notions:
Tapestry needle
Stitch marker
14-inch round pillow
form or fiberfill
Dressmaker's chalk

Finished size:
14 inches diameter

Gauge:
Double crochet 14
stitches and 7½ rows
equals 4 inches.
Gauge is not critical,
but front and back
should be the same
size. If your gauge
with the different
yarn varies, you may
need to work different
numbers of rounds
for each.

Front:

With A, ch 4. Join with sl st to form circle.

R1: Ch 3 (counts as 1 dc). Work 11 dc in ring. Join with sl st to first dc (12 dc).

R2: Ch 3 (counts as first dc of round here and throughout). 2 dc in each dc. Join with sl st to first dc (24 dc).

R3: Ch 3. 1 dc in next dc. *2 dc in next dc, 1 dc in next dc, rep from * around. End with 2 dc in final dc. Join with sl st to first dc (36 dc).

R4: Ch 3. 1 dc in next dc. *2 dc in next dc, 1 dc in next 2 dc, rep from * around. End with 2 dc in final dc. Join with sl st to first dc (48 dc).

R5: Ch 3. 1 dc in next 2 dc. *2 dc in next dc, 1 dc in next 3 dc, rep from * around. End with 2 dc in final dc. Join with sl st to first dc (60 dc).

R6: Ch 3. 1 dc in next 3 dc. *2 dc in next dc, 1 dc in next 4 dc, rep from * around. End with 2 dc in final dc. Join with sl st to first dc (72 dc).

R7: Ch 3. 1 dc in next 4 dc. *2 dc in next dc, 1 dc in next 5 dc, rep from * around. End with 2 dc in final dc. Join with sl st to first dc (84 dc).

R8: Ch 3. 1 dc in next 5 dc. *2 dc in next dc, 1 dc in next 6 dc, rep from * around. End with 2 dc in final dc. Join with sl st to first dc (96 dc).

R9: Ch 3. 1 dc in next 6 dc. *2 dc in next dc, 1 dc in next 7 dc, rep from * around. End with 2 dc in final dc. Join with sl st to first dc (108 dc).

R10: Ch 3. 1 dc in next 7 dc. *2 dc in next dc, 1 dc in next 8 dc, rep from * around. End with 2 dc in final dc. Join with sl st to first dc (120 dc).

R11: Ch 3. 1 dc in next 8 dc. *2 dc in next dc, 1 dc in next 9 dc, rep from * around. End with 2 dc in final dc. Join with sl st to first dc (132 dc).

The back of the pillow is almost as pretty as the front!

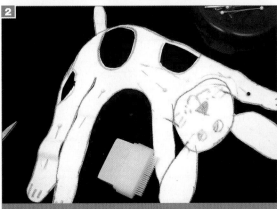

Pin the pattern on the front of the pillow, and trace with chalk.

Follow the chalk line with chain stitch.

R12: Ch 3. 1 dc in next 9 dc. *2 dc in next dc, 1 dc in next 10 dc, rep from * around. End with 2 dc in final dc. Join with sl st to first dc (144 dc).

R13: Ch 3. 1 dc in next 10 dc. *2 dc in next dc, 1 dc in next 11 dc, rep from * around. End with 2 dc in final dc. Join with sl st to first dc (156 dc).

Back:

Make same as for front, using B. If using the color-changing yarn suggested, work in a spiral. (Do not join at end of rounds; place a stitch marker at the beginning of the round and move at each round.) At end of last round, work 1 dc, 1 hdc, 1 sc, 1 sl st. Cut yarn.

Working gradually, decreasing stitches on the last round of a spiral eases the edge into a circle. (See Chapter 2 for more on circles and spirals.)

Block the front and back. (See Chapter 2 for blocking instructions.)

Now for the fun part: putting the drawing on the pillow. If necessary, size your child's drawing to fit the front of the pillow using a scanner or photocopier. Cut out copy (not the original!) and lay over front of pillow. Outline the drawing with dressmaker's chalk.

Using B, chain stitch around the outline, unwinding the color-changing yarn to the desired color, if necessary.

4. Fill in spots with satin stitch, making long stitches across the space to be filled.

5. Sew on the facial features.

Tail:

The tail and ears of the dog are worked separately and sewn on.

Ch 6. Sc in second ch from hook. Hdc in next ch. Dc in next 3 ch. Cut yarn. Position at tail spot, pull both ends through, and tie together on back.

If you're adapting your own design, choose elements to "pop" in 3D by crocheting the parts and attaching them to the pillow, as I've done with the ears and tail here.

Ears (make 2):

Ch 9. Sc in second ch from hook. Hdc in next ch. Dc in next 5 ch. 2hdc in last ch. Working up back side of ch: 5 dc, 1 hdc, 1 sc. Pull yarn through and cut, leaving a tail for sewing. Sew ears on at ear position.

Finishing:

Place the front and back wrong sides together, and pin at increases.

Satin stitch details like the spots.

Have fun embroidering the face.

Pin the sides at the increases and single crochet together.

6 **R1:** Join B at edge and sc around. If you have a pillow form, insert it when you get halfway round and then continue sc sides together. If you're stuffing with fiberfill, work about $\frac{3}{4}$ way around, stuff , and finish sc around edge. Join with sl st to first sc.

R2: Work 1 row of crab stitch (reverse single crochet). At the end, join with sl st to first crab st. Cut yarn. Weave in ends.

Make It Your Own

This design seemed well suited to a round "canvas," but make whatever shape—square, rectangle, hexagon—best suits the work of your little *artiste*. Let your child pick the colors, even if you think they're outrageous. You can work a more elaborate border if you like. See more edgings in Chapter 12.

More Fun Stuff

In This Chapter

Throw your own party with the
Party Hat

Keep cool with
The World's Best Ice-Cream Cozy

Get some shut-eye with the
Incredible Rose-Colored Sleep Glasses

Treat your feline friends with
Kitty Bonbons

You could probably live a complete life without the projects in this chapter—but why would you want to? These projects make things more fun. From a festive party hat to cool sleep goggles, a cozy for your ice cream and toys for your kitty—this lively stuff is all easy enough to make for yourself and some worthy friends.

Sure, you can go the traditional route at parties and wear a lampshade. But this hat lets folks know who the party person is. Or keep it in the family, by making one for the birthday kid (big or little) to wear on his or her special day. Birthday cake will wash right off this acrylic yarn, which is used double to let the hat stand up on its own.

Bring on the party with the Party Hat!

Party Hat

Skill level:
11

Yarn:

Red Heart Super Saver
Multicolor (100%
acrylic, 5 oz., 278 yd.),
1 skein Bikini 0929 (A);
Lion Fun Fur (100%
polyester, 50 g, 60 yd.),
1 ball Turquoise 320-
148 (B)

Crochet hook:

K (6.5mm)

Notions:

Tapestry needle
Sewing needle
Thread
Stitch marker
4 feet (1-inch-wide)
ribbon, to coordinate
with yarn

Finished size:

21 inches in circumfer-
ence by 8½ inches tall

Gauge:

Double crochet 10
stitches and 6 rows
equals 4 inches

Just a reminder: the Bikini yarn is used doubled
throughout this project. And this hat is a good excuse to
get out and use your stitch markers. Put one in the first
stitch of each round, and move it up with each row.

To use yarn doubled, pull one end from the center of the
skein and the other end from the outside of the skein.
Hold the ends together and crochet as if they are a single
strand.

With A doubled, ch 54. Join to first ch with a sl st, being
careful not to twist.

R1: Sc around (54 sc).

R2: *Sc 7, sc 2 tog, rep from * around (48 sc).

R3: Dc around.

R4: *Sc 6, sc 2 tog, rep from * around (42 sc).

R5: Dc around.

R6: *Sc 5, sc 2 tog, rep from * around (36 sc).

R7: Dc around.

R8: *Sc 4, sc 2 tog, rep from * around (30 sc).

R9: Dc around.

R10: *Sc 3, sc 2 tog, rep from * around (24 sc).

R11: Dc around.

R12: *Sc 2, sc 2 tog, rep from * around (18 sc).

R13: Dc around.

R14: *Sc 1, sc 2 tog, rep from * around (12 sc).

R15: Dc around.

R16: *Sc 2 tog, rep from * around (6 sc).

R17: *Sc 2 tog, rep from * around (3 sc).

Yarn over and pull loop through final loop. Cut, leaving
a tail. Use tail to tidy up ends on tip, pull end through
tip to inside, and weave in.

Single crochet the Fun Fur around the edge for a little sparkle.

Sew the ribbons to the sides of the hat. These will help keep the hat on your partying head.

1. To make edging, join B, doubled, at edge of hat. Sc around.

   Weave in ends. Gently tug out ends of Fun Fur for a fluffier fringe.

2. Cut 2 (24-inch) lengths of ribbon. Using sewing thread, sew to each side of hat.

Many ribbons are wont to fray when cut. To help keep the ribbon from fraying, fold the end over and sew along the fold.

Make It Your Own

Not enough bling? Add a pompom on top. As always, use the colors that speak to you. To make a smaller hat, decrease by 6 chains and after row 1, start with row 4. This will make the hat shorter, too.

The World's Best Ice Cream Cozy

This cozy was inspired by my brother, who has a serious ice-cream monkey. He can kick back a pint of Ben & Jerry's like some folks kick back a pint of lager. To keep him from freezing his fingers and to insulate the ice cream, I made him a wool ice-cream cozy. And because, occasionally, he has to take a little break before he finishes it all, I made him a lanyard and spoon holder to keep his ice cream close while he takes a nap.

Skill level:
/ / /

Yarn:
Noro Kureyon (100% wool, 50 g, 100 m), 1 ball color 102 (A); Patons Classic Wool (100% wool, 3.5 oz., 223 yd.), small amount black (B)

Crochet hook:
I (5.5mm)

Notions:
Tapestry needle

Finished size:
11 inches in circumference by 3½ inches tall

Gauge:
In single-crochet rib stitch, unstretched, 16 stitches and 12 rows equals 4 inches

The World's Best Ice-Cream Cozy—looks yummy, doesn't it?

Slip stitch the sides together.

For the bottom edge, single-crochet in the "ditch."

Make It Your Own

If your ice-cream craze isn't as intense as my brother's, leave off the lanyard and spoon holder. If you prefer the heftier quart size, make the starting chain long enough to reach top to bottom, minus 1 inch (to allow for edging) and then add enough rows to wrap around—best leave off the lanyard, lest you hurt your neck. If you're into those rectangular half-gallons, you might consider a 12-step program.

Kureyon has a rainbow of colors. Want to use that purple a few yards away? Just wind off the yarn and break it at the point you want.

With A, ch 12.

R1: Sc in second ch and in every ch across (11 sc). Turn.

R2–30: Ch 1. *Working in back loop only,* sc across. Turn.

Do not cut yarn on final row.

Depending on your gauge, you might need more or fewer rows. Wrap the cozy around the pint, stretching just a bit (it should "hug" the ice cream container). When it fits, stop.

1 Sl st the last row to first row.

Top edge:

Join B at one edge.

R1: Work sc evenly around.

R2: Work crab stitch (reverse single crochet) around.

Bottom edge:

2 Join B at other edge. Work 1 sc in each "ditch" formed between ridges. (This will make the bottom edge snug so the pint doesn't fall out!)

Lanyard:

Join B at any point on the top edge. Work ch st to desired length to fit over head and around neck. Attach with sl st to the first sc. This is now the back of the cozy.

Spoon holder:

Join B at top edge on side. Ch 5. Join at starting point.

Weave in all ends. Dig in!

Incredible Rose-Colored Sleep Glasses

Slip on these Incredible Rose-Colored Sleep Glasses, and you'll be in dreamland in no time. The yarn is the ever-soothing Calmer by Rowan. The diving mask–style back fits snugly and lets you avoid the knotty headache you can get from tie-on masks. And as if they couldn't get better: you can make these in the time it takes to brew up and sip some Sleepytime tea.

Skill level:
/ / /

Yarn:
Rowan Calmer (75% cotton, 25% acrylic microfiber, 50 g, 175 yd.), 1 ball each Blush 477 (A), Onyx 465 (B)

Crochet hook:
G

Notions:
Tapestry needle

Finished size:
20 inches in circumference; eyepiece is 2½ inches in diameter

Gauge:
The whole thing is smaller than a gauge swatch! Just crochet a circle and be sure it covers your eye.

Dreamland beckons you ... slip on the Incredible Rose-Colored Sleep Glasses ....

Here's what the back of the diving mask-style looks like.

Begin the side panel.

The Calmer yarn is both super-soft and somewhat elastic. If you substitute a yarn, first hold it to your eyelid to be sure it won't itch. If it does and you want to use it anyway, sew a soft backing under the eye part.

Eye glasses:

With A, ch 2.

R1: In second ch from hook, sc 6. Join with sl st to first ch. Do not turn.

R2: Ch 1. 2 sc in each sc around. Join with sl st to first ch (12 sc).

R3: Ch 1. *1 sc in next sc, 2 sc in next sc, rep from * around. Join with sl st to first ch (18 sc).

R4: Ch 1. *1 sc in next 2 sc, 2 sc in next sc, rep from * around. Join with sl st to first ch (24 sc).

R5: Ch 1. *1 sc in next 3 sc, 2 sc in next sc, rep from * around. Join with sl st to first ch (30 sc).

R6: Join B with ch. *1 sc in next 4 sc, 2 sc in next sc, rep from * around. Join with sl st to first ch (36 sc).

Strap:

R7: Sc 2 tog. Sc in next 3 sc, 2 sc in next sc, sc in next 3 sc, sc 2 tog. Turn.

R8: Ch 1. Sc 2 tog. Sc in next 2 sc, 2 sc in next sc, sc in next 3 sc, sc 2 tog. Turn.

Because of the center increase, the rows are briefly asymmetrical. They will end up even.

R9: Ch 1. Sc 2 tog. Sc in next 2 sc, 2 sc in next sc, sc in next 2 sc, sc 2 tog. Turn.

R10: Ch 1. Sc 2 tog. Sc in next 2 sc, 2 sc in next sc, sc in next 1 sc, sc 2 tog. Turn.

R11: Ch 1. Sc 2 tog. Sc in next sc, 2 sc in next sc, sc in next sc, sc 2 tog. Turn.

R12: Ch 1. Sc 2 tog. Sc in next 2 sc, sc 2 tog. Turn.

R13–26: Ch 1. Sc in 4 sc. Turn.

R 27: Ch 1. Sc in first 2 sc. Turn.

Stop! Before you go on, check that your narrow strap is on the right side. With right side of glasses up, be sure each narrow strap has a "notch" to fit into on the other side. If not, just crochet one more row of 4 single crochets on narrow strap so the narrow strap lines up.

R28–42: Ch 1. Sc in 2 sc. Turn.

When you reach the end, cut the yarn, leaving a 24-inch tail.

Repeat rows 1 through 42 to make second half of glasses.

Joining:

2 With same side of goggles facing up, pin narrow straps to the corresponding "notch" on the other side. Sl st the narrow strap into notch. Repeat for other narrow strap.

Before sewing together, pin the straps and nose bridge together to make sure it's a good fit—it should fit snugly without binding or flopping. Add or subtract rows evenly on both sides until it fits. Also, be sure the eye patches have the same side up and the straps aren't twisted.

3 With right sides facing, sl st across center 5 sts at bridge of nose.

Cut yarn. Weave in ends. Slip on Sleep Glasses. Doze off.

Make It Your Own

You could, if you wanted, make these in green and be the Green Hornet.

Join narrow part of strap to "notch."

Slip stitch across the center of the bridge of the glasses.

What kitty doesn't dream of sitting on a tuffet nibbling on bonbons? Make your kitty's dreams come true with these yummy cat treats stuffed with catnip and/or fiberfill. If you don't have a kitty, you could stuff these with lavender and slip them into your lingerie drawer—or into someone's gift basket. Or go get yourself a kitty.

Life is like a box of ... Kitty Bonbons.

Note: Substitute any color you like, but stick with cotton, which has low shed, so kitty doesn't develop digestive complications.

Kitty Bonbons

Sweetsie

A Sweetsie for your sweetie (feline sweetie, that is).

Skill level:
///

Yarn:
Peaches and Creme (100% cotton, 2.5 oz., 150 yd.), small amount Black Cherry 198 (A), Shocking Pink 31 (B)

Crochet hook:
H (5mm)

Notions:
Tapestry needle
Fiberfill
Catnip (or your choice of filling)

Finished size:
4½ inches wide by 4½ inches around

Gauge:
Varies

Truffle

Kitty will have fun batting around this Truffle.

Skill level:
///

Yarn:
Sugar and Cream (100% cotton, 2.5 oz., 120 yd.), Warm Brown 1130 (A); Peaches and Creme (100% cotton, 2.5 oz., 150 yd.), small amount Shocking Pink 31 (B).

Crochet hook:
H (5mm)

Notions:
Tapestry needle
Fiberfill
Catnip (or your choice of filling)

Finished size:
2 inches wide by 7½ inches around

Gauge:
Varies

Nougat

More than likely, you'll find this Nougat treat batted under the sofa soon after presenting it to kitty.

Skill level:
///

Yarn:
Sugar and Cream (100% cotton, 2.5 oz., 120 yd.), Warm Brown 1130 (A), White 1 (B); Peaches and Creme (100% cotton, 2.5 oz., 150 yd.), Shocking Pink 31 (C)

Crochet hook:
H (5mm)

Notions:
Tapestry needle
Fiberfill
Catnip (or your choice of filling)

Finished size:
3 inches wide by 2 inches tall

Gauge:
Varies

Work the frills across the short ends of the rectangle.

Sew the long sides together.

Weave thread through the eyelets.

Sweetsie

With A, ch 11.

R1: Sc in second ch from hook and in each ch across (10 sc). Turn.

R2–12: Ch 1, sc across. End. Cut yarn, leaving an 18-inch tail for sewing.

Frills:

R1: Join B at right side of one short end. Sc 12 evenly across. Turn.

R2: Ch. 4 (counts as 1 dc and ch 1). *Sk 1 sc. Dc in next sc, ch 1, rep from * across, ending with dc in final sc (7 dc, 6 ch-1 spaces). Turn.

R3: Ch 1. Sc in each dc and each ch-1 space, ending with 1 sc in ch-4 space (12 sc). Turn.

R4: *Ch 1, sc in next sc, ch 3 rep from *, ending with sc in final sc (12 sc). End, leaving 12-inch tail.

Repeat on other short side.

Assembly:

With A, cut 2 (6-inch) pieces.

Sew up long side of candy. Weave 2 lengths of A through eyelets on ends. Pull one end taut, and tie a knot in the string. Stuff piece with fiberfill and/or catnip. Pull second end taut, and tie a knot.

Truffle

With A, ch 2.

R1: In second ch from hook, work 6 sc. Do not join.

R2: Work 2 sc in each sc around (12 sc).

R3: Work 2 sc in each sc around (24 sc).

R4–10: Work 1 sc in each sc around.

Intermission: spiral chain:

4 Join B at starting st, with end of yarn inside truffle. Working along the spiral formed by the single crochets, work chain stitch to desired length; see photos for a pattern guide. Cut yarn and pull to the **5** inside. Tie ends of A and B into a knot.

Read more about chain stitching on the surface in Chapter 12.

R11: Working in back loop only, sc around.

R12: Sc 2 tog around.

Stuff truffle.

R13: Sc 2 tog around.

R14: Sc 2 tog around. Cut yarn. Weave yarn through center stitches and pull tight.

Nougat

With A, ch 17.

R1: Sc in second ch and each ch across (16 sc). Turn.

R2: Ch 1. Sc across, joining B in loop of final sc (16 sc). Turn.

R3: Ch 1. With B, work sc across (16 sc). Turn.

R4: Ch 1. Sc across, joining C in loop of final sc (16 sc). Turn.

R5: Ch 1. With C, work sc across (16 sc). Turn.

R6: Sl st across first 4 sc. Work 8 sc (8 sc). Note: 4 sts are left unworked. Turn.

R7–11: Ch 1, sc across (8 sc).

R12: Ch 1, sc across, joining B in loop of final sc (8 sc). Turn.

Working with the yarn on the inside, chain stitch along the spiral.

Secure the chain end and pull it to the inside.

You now have a T-shaped object.

Sew 4 rows of pink to the short side rows of pink.

Turn and sew 2 rows of pink to the long side of the nougat.

R13: Ch 1, sc across (8 sc). Turn.

R14: Ch 1, sc across, joining A in loop of final sc (8 sc). Turn.

R15–20: Ch 1. With A, sc across (8 sc). Turn.

At end of row 20, cut yarn, leaving a long tail.

Assembly:

6 You now have a T-shaped object, which you are going to sew into a box shape. Bend the T at the long bar and, using a

7 whipstitch, sew 4 rows of the long bar to the 4 rows of a cross-bar.

8 This leaves 2 rows of pink unsewn. Wrap these 2 rows around the edge and sew in place. Repeat on other side. Use a white tail to sew the white lines together. Use a long brown tail to sew the brown segment. Match 2 rows on side, wrap and sew 4 rows across the end, and sew halfway down the long side. Repeat on other side, stopping before finishing long side.

You'll be sewing on the wrong side, so don't worry about the ends. They'll be tucked in, out of sight, when you turn it right side out.

Turn right side out, leaving all those pesky ends inside the nougat. Stuff and then finish sewing long side.

Make It Your Own

Make this sweet stuff in whatever colors tickle your kitty's fancy. You can run a string through them and tie them to a stick if you want to really get your cat excited.

Beyond the Basics

In Part 4, I take crochet to the next level, beyond patterns and into the realm of your own imagination. First, crochet buddies up to knitting to enhance cuffs, collars, and surfaces. And hardware store washers meet thread and beads to create buttons that enhance just about anything!

There's not much in the way of traditional patterns in the following pages. Rather, you'll find basic methods that serve as gateways for your own creations. It's tons of fun, so pick up your hook and get ready to explore!

Crochet for Knitters

In This Chapter

Fixing—and making—holes

Finishing off knitted edges with crochet stitches

Embellishing your knitted pieces with crochet

Simply marvelous buttons

Knitters can find a lot to love about crochet. Crochet can fix a dropped stitch or a curling edge. Crochet can put a fine edging around a neckline, shoulder, or cuff in a fraction of the time it takes to knit. In fact, crochet can add such fancy embellishments as shells or picots without pain. Crochet's sturdiness lends itself to really fine buttonholes. And it makes fabulous buttons! So put down those knitting needles for a bit and pick up a crochet hook!

Picking Up Stitches

Whoops! Dropped a stitch! Grab your crochet hook, stick it into the loop, and pull the rogue loop back onto your knitting needle. If the loop escapes down a row or so, stick the hook into the loop and use the hook to latch onto the horizontal bar of the stitch above it. Pull this through the loop on the hook. Continue pulling loops through 1 row at a time until you get back to the live row. Pull the final loop onto your needle.

Pick up the dropped loop and then pick up the horizontal bar above it and pull through.

If you don't already have a crochet hook, get a size G or H to stash in your knitting bag.

You can also use a crochet hook to help pick up stitches around a neckline or cuff. Just use the hook to pick up the stitches, 10 at a time, and slide the loops onto the knitting needle. (Or just crochet the edging! See directions later in this chapter.) Use a crochet hook with a plain handle, not one of those fancy hooks with the padded handle, so the loops can slide down it. Use a hook with a handle similar in size to the knitting needle.

Use a crochet hook to help pick up stitches to knit around an edge.

Ready to cable and can't find your cable needle? You can use the handle of a crochet hook as a cable needle. Just slide the handle in to hold the stitches, and when you're ready, slide the stitches back onto the needle and knit them off.

Don't try to knit the stitches directly off the crochet hook, because it's not pointy enough and the stitches will fall off.

On Edge

I love knitting. But when I read these directions:

> *Pick up 113 stitches evenly around neckline. Bind off.*

I break into a sweat. In addition to the peskiness of picking up the stitches, there's the added terror of not picking them up evenly. When this happens, you get a wonky edge, so you have to pull out, start over, sweat some more. Or you can skip the angst and just crochet on an edge. This is also a good way to "straighten" a curling edge on a scarf or an uneven edge on a sweater.

Single Crochet Edge

To crochet on a single crochet edge, insert your hook in a corner stitch and connect with a slip stitch. Work single crochets evenly around the edge, working extras if necessary around the corners.

A single crochet edge.

Crab Stitch (Reverse Single Crochet) Edge

To crochet on a crab stitch edge, work one row of single crochet. Do not turn. Insert your hook in the last single crochet made, and work single crochet. Make a single crochet in the stitch to the right of your hook and then continue across, working from left to right.

A crab stitch edge.

Loop Edge

To crochet on a loop edge, single crochet. *Chain 3, skip one stitch, single crochet, and repeat from * to end.

When you skip 1 stitch, skip the distance equivalent to 1 single crochet, which might be more than 1 knit stitch. When evenly spaced, the work should lie flat.

A loop edge.

A double crochet loop edge.

A picot stitch edge.

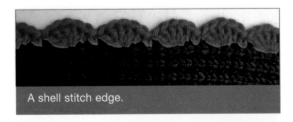
A shell stitch edge.

A wavy edge.

Double Crochet Loop Edge

To crochet a double crochet loop edge, work 1 row of single crochet evenly. Turn. Chain 1, *double crochet, chain 3, skip 1 stitch, double crochet in the next stitch, and rep from * to end.

Picot Stitch Edge

To crochet a picot stitch edge, *single crochet, (chain 3, join with slip stitch in the third chain from your hook), skip 1 stitch, and repeat from * around, ending with 1 sc.

Shell Stitch Edge

To crochet a shell stitch edge, single crochet, *skip 1 stitch, make 5 double crochets in the next stitch, skip 1 stitch, make 1 single crochet, and repeat from * around.

Wavy Edge

To crochet a wavy edge, work 1 each of these stitches along the edge: *slip stitch, single crochet, half-double crochet, double crochet, triple crochet, double crochet, half-double crochet, single crochet, and repeat from *.

Beaded Edge

To crochet a beaded edge, string the beads onto your yarn. With the front side up, work a base row of evenly spaced single crochets. Turn. Chain 1. Single crochet. *Slide the desired number of beads (my sample shown in the following photo uses 8) up to your hook. Single crochet in next 2 single crochets. Repeat from *. End with single crochet in the final single crochet.

Work with wrong side of knitted fabric facing you, as the beads will "pop" to the front.

A beaded edge.

Slide the beads up and then single crochet into the next stitch.

Surface Designs

Why surface embellishment? It's a fabulous way to add lushness to pillow or pocketbooks. In a very light mohair, it's an interesting but not overwhelming design element for sweaters or skirts. (In a heavier yarn, you run the risk of looking like a toilet-tissue cover.) And surface embellishment is great for adding some fun to kids' hats, but be judicious in sweater use, so your child doesn't look like an elaborately frosted cake.

This knitted lace cotton vest features chain stitch embellishment and single-crochet edging in variegated silk.

This chain stitch is in silk on cotton.

Working the chain stitch, with the yarn held under the knitting.

Working the chain stitch, with the yarn held under the knitting.

Chain Stitch Embellishment

Chain stitch is a fine choice for freeform designs. You can either hold the yarn under the fabric and pull it through or work with the yarn on top of the fabric. Working with the yarn on top is best suited to linear designs because the yarn will create a parallel "echo" line next to the chain stitches. This fine for lines, but not so fine for curves, which will end up with a wide echo. The surface line is nearly invisible when you work "in the ditch" between rib rows. The advantage here is that the yarn won't show on the back of the fabric. For curvy designs, hold the yarn underneath. Note that the yarn will show on the back of the fabric, looking like a running stitch.

Whether you work with the yarn on top or under the fabric, be sure to secure the yarns ends when you're done.

You can "sketch out" a design by laying a piece of yarn in the desired line across the fabric and then crocheting next to it. Don't sweat it; this is not an exact science.

"Sketch" a design with a piece of yarn ....

... and then crochet next to the design.

Double Crochet Embellishment

To add a double crochet embellishment, insert your hook in the fabric, working your hook under a horizontal bar, and join with a slip stitch. Work double crochets across the surface of fabric in your desired pattern. To make working easier, fold the fabric along the line to be worked; you'll be able to see bars to work under.

A double crochet swerve.

Fold fabric to work surface crochet. Insert hook under bar of knit stitch.

A shell stitch swerve.

Shell Stitch Embellishment

To add a shell stitch embellishment, join your yarn with a slip stitch, being sure to catch the horizontal bar. *Work 1 single crochet, skip 1 stitch, work 5 double crochets into the next stitch. Repeat from *, working along the desired pattern line.

Button It Up

A crocheted button adds a fine finishing touch to a fiber garment, whether it's knitted, crocheted, or woven. And all of them, even the beaded button, take very little time to make.

A bunch of buttons.

Sushi Buttons

If you made the Sushi Crochet Hook Roll-Up in Chapter 3, use the leftover yarn to make these buttons. An advantage of using a button base rather than stuffing is that you have a shank to sew the button on, so it's more stable.

Have fun fixing up these Sushi Buttons.

Skill level:
111

Yarn:
There are 3 choices for A. Choose 1 or make a set. Kristin Nicholas Julia (50% wool, 25% kid mohair, 25% alpaca, 50 g, 93 yd.), small amount each Carrot 2250 (A), Harvest Gold 2163 (A), or Spring Green 585 (A); Natural 0010 (B); Velvet Moss 6086 (C)

Crochet hook:
G (4.25mm)

Notions:
Tapestry needle
Fray Check or glue
1-inch diameter button *or* fiberfill

Finished size:
$1\frac{3}{8}$ inches in diameter

Gauge:
Varies. Just be sure your stitches are tight enough to hide the button you're covering.

Any button—ugly or pretty—works here.

Weave in the ends on the back side.

Sew the cover onto the button.

You can use a regular old button for this project—preferably an unattractive one that could use a slipcover.

For a larger button, add another increase row (single crochet in 2 single crochets, 2 single crochets in the next single crochet). For a smaller button, skip an increase row. If you use a deeper button as a base, add a plain row without increases before the decrease.

With A, ch 2.

R1: In second ch from hook, sc 6. Pull tail to close hole. Join to first sc with sl st. Do not turn.

R2: Ch 1. Join B. Work 2 sc in each sc. Join to first sc with sl st (12 sc).

R3: Join C. *Sc in 1 sc, 2 sc in next sc. rep from * around. Join to first sc with sl st (18 sc).

R4: Ch 1. Sc around.(18 sc). Join to first sc with sl st.

R5: Ch 1. *Sk 1 sc, sc in next sc, rep from * around (9 sc).

Do not cut yarn.

1. Turn the button cover inside out and weave in the ends. Snip the yarn ends and dab Fray Check or glue on top of the ends to keep them from unraveling. Let dry.

R6: Insert button. Sc in second sc from hook and in every other sc around (5 sc). Cut yarn, leaving a longish tail.

2. Use the tail to secure the button cover to the button. Do not cover shank.

Ringie Dingies

These buttons use ordinary washers from the hardware store. Buy a bundle in various sizes and experiment with your own styles!

One Ringie Dingie, two Ringie Dingie.

One Ringie Dingie:

Join A around ¾-inch washer with a slip stitch. Insert your hook in the center of the washer and pull up the loop. Pull even to the edge of the washer. Yarn over and pull loop through both loops on hook. That's 1 single crochet made. Continue to single crochet around the washer until it's covered. Join with a slip stitch to the first single crochet.

1

Crochet around the washer.

Skill level:
/ / /

Yarn:
Royale Fashion Crochet Thread Size 3 (100% mercerized cotton, 150 yd.), small amount Warm Teal 65 (A), Warm Rose 775 (B)

Crochet hook:
D

Notions:
Tapestry needle
Beading needle
Washers: ¾ inch with ½ inch center hole (for A), 1 inch with ⅝-inch center hole (for B)
25 to 30 (2mm) beads (for B)
Fray Check or glue

Finished size:
1⅓ inch diameter (A) and 1¼ inch diameter (B)

Gauge:
Varies.

Chain 3, and slip stitch into the back loop of the next stitch.

Slide the bead next to the single crochet and chain around it.

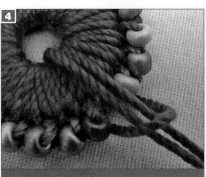

Slip a loop around the washer, and use with a loop buttonhole.

Use a Ringie Dingie as a frame for a smaller button.

2 To work picot edge, slip stitch in the back loop of the first single crochet, *chain 3, slip stitch in the back loop of the next single crochet, and repeat from * around. Cut thread, leaving a long tail.

Weave thread under thread behind washer. Secure ends with a dab of Fray Check or glue.

Two Ringie Dingie:

Thread beads onto B. Join B around 1-inch washer with a slip stitch. *Insert your hook in the center of the washer and pull up the loop. Pull even to edge of washer. Yarn over and pull the loop through both loops on your hook. That's 1 single crochet made.

3 Slide a bead up to the single crochet. Make a chain to secure the bead. Repeat from * until washer is covered. Cut thread, leaving a long tail.

String on more beads than you think you'll need. If you get caught short, you'll have to start over!

Weave thread under thread behind washer. Secure ends with a dab of Fray Check or glue.

4 To use a Ringie Dingie, loop a string around the ring and tie the other end to the garment or bag. Let it dangle through a loop buttonhole.

5 Or you could use the Ringie Dingie as a "charger" or frame for a smaller button. Slip the shank through the center hole and sew the shank to the desired place.

Button Doily

Take a button to the next level with a fancy button cover. This works best with a brightly colored button that shows through the lacy crocheted cover.

Dress up a button with a crocheted Button Doily.

Skill level:
11

Yarn:
DMC Cotton Perle size 5 (100% cotton, 25 yd.), 1 skein blue or desired color

Crochet hook:
1 (2.75mm)

Notions:
Tapestry needle

Finished size:
1.2 inch diameter

Gauge:
Varies.

Ch 4. Join with sl st.

R1: Ch 5 (counts as tr and ch-1). In ring, work (tr, ch-1) 14 times (15 tr). Join with sl st to ch-4 of starting ch.

R2: Ch 3. Dc in every tr and every ch-1 space around (30 dc). Join with sl st to starting ch.

R3: Ch 1. Sc in second dc from hook and in every other dc around (15 sc). Do not cut thread.

Insert the button and crochet the back closed.

Be sure to not cover the shank!

Turn button cover inside out and weave in ends. Snip yarn ends and dab Fray Check or glue on top of the ends. Let dry.

1 **R4:** Insert button. Sc in second sc from hook and in every other sc around (8 sc). Cut thread, leaving a longish tail.

Use tail to secure button cover to button.

2 Do not cover shank.

Buttonholes

Sometimes a knitted buttonhole turns out too loose to do its job well. A crocheted edging can firm it up. Just crochet around the edge of the buttonhole using single crochet or reverse single crochet.

Make the buttonhole a design element by using a contrasting color and/or yarn.

You can crochet buttonholes onto knitted garments, too. You work the loop buttonhole and the covered loop on the edge, rather than into the buttonhole band.

The loop buttonhole works well with little buttons that won't take much stress, and it's best worked in conjunction with a crocheted border. To make in conjunction with a single crochet edging, at the desired buttonhole point, chain 5. Rejoin with single crochet in next the single crochet.

A sturdier loop is the covered buttonhole. You can work this in conjunction with a crocheted edging or add it on by itself. Mark ½-inch space to make the buttonhole. With the wrong side facing you, attach the yarn at the bottom of the space. Chain 8. Reattach the yarn with a slip stitch at the top of the ½-inch space. Turn. Single crochet over the chain until it's covered. Attach with slip stitch at the base of the chain loop. Cut yarn, leaving a tail. Using tail, whipstitch at both sides of the loop to reinforce. Weave in ends.

Got a droopy buttonhole?

Reinforce it with a row of single crochet.

For a loop buttonhole, chain stitch to make loop and then rejoin to the edging.

To make a stronger buttonhole, single crochet around a chain worked from the bottom to the top.

Free-for-All

In This Chapter

Dress up your ears with the
Hyperbole Earrings

Whip up the yummy
Olive Love Bowl

Get All Wrapped Up
with your test pieces

My goal up to this point was to write clear instructions for you to create the projects featured in these pages—with some additional notes on how to make a project your own. This chapter is a real celebration of "making it your own," drawing on all your crochet skills you've learned so far to create utterly unique projects. I provide some techniques and sample projects. I hope you take these tools and run for the rainbow of your own creativity. Nearly all of these projects rely on materials that you already have—scraps of yarn and bits of practice crochet. Free your inner crocheter!

These wee Hyperbole Earrings are not for the faint of heart!

Hyperboles

Unleash your inner crochet geek! Mathematician (and crocheter) Daina Taimina developed this crocheted model of the hyperbolic plane in an effort to physically represent a plane on which space curves away at every point. This fascinating representation of a previously unviewable geometric concept rocked the mathematical world.

And you—yes, you—can create your own hyperbolic plane. As with most known things, once it is defined, creating it as well as making it your own is easy.

To read more about Taimina and the hyperbolic plane, see www.cabinetmagazine.org/issues/16/crocheting.php and www.theiff.org/oexhibits/oe1e.html.

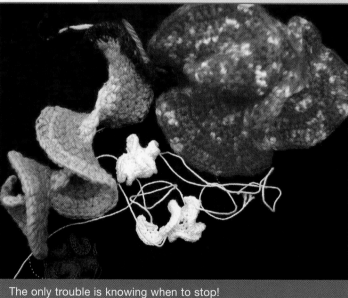

The only trouble is knowing when to stop!

Your Own Hyperbolic Plane

The hyperbolic plane is made by single crocheting at a tight gauge and increasing at regular intervals. You get to decide how frequently you want to increase. More than 6 will take several rows to see the full effect. The models shown are *N4* and *N3* models—increasing every fourth stitch and third stitch, respectively. The earrings (coming up) increase every stitch.

N3, 7 rows.

N4, 11 rows.

Skill level:
11

Yarn:
Use a fairly taut yarn; worsted weight is best. Fuzzy yarns won't work well. The N4 model uses Red Heart Super Saver Multicolor (100% acrylic, 5 oz., 278 yd.), Sunshine Print 9798; the N3 model uses Noro Cotton Kureyon (70% cotton, 30% wool, 50 g, 100 m), 1 skein color 14

Crochet hook:
Use one much smaller than called for; C or D with worsted weight is about right

Notions:
Tapestry needle

Finished size:
Your choice

Gauge:
Varies.

Crocheting worsted weight with a hook designed for fingering weight is tough on the tendons. Be sure to rest your hand between rows.

Ch a multiple of N, plus 1 chain for turning. The N4 shown has a starting chain of 21 ($20 = 4 \times 5 + 1$). The N3 model has a starting chain of 22 ($21 = 3 \times 7 + 1$).

R1: Sc in second ch from hook. Sc across, working 2 sc in the Nth chain (for N3: sc in 2 ch, 2 sc in third ch; repeat to end of row). At end, turn.

R2: Ch 1. Sc across, working 2 sc in the Nth sc. If you have extra sc's at the end, work just one sc in each. Turn.

Remaining rows: Repeat row 2 for the pattern, with your choice on the number of rows. You'll get a pleasing swerve by the third row, which intensifies by the sixth row. At about the tenth row, it begins curving in the other direction. And beyond that, it continues swerving to then fro. Keep crocheting until you like the shape—or until your wrist cries "Uncle!"

Make It Your Own

It might be fun to do the final row in Fun Fur.

Hyperbole Earrings

These earrings are an N1, which swerves quite dramatically and quickly. It has only 8 rows, but they're intense.

The Hyperbole Earrings are just 1¼ inches across.

Skill level:
111

Yarn:
South Main Crochet Thread Size 10 (100% cotton, 350 yd.), 1 ball each Victory Red 494 and Purple 458

Crochet hook:
Size 10 steel hook

Notions:
Tapestry needle
Earring hooks

Finished size:
1¼ inches

Gauge:
Varies.

Sew the wee seam.

You might want to choose a closed earring wire so your precious planes don't fly off the wire!

With A, ch 2.

R1: In second ch from hook, sc 1 (2 sc). Turn.

R2: Ch 1. 2 sc in each sc (4 sc). Turn.

R3: Ch 1. 2 sc in each sc (8 sc). Turn.

R4: Ch 1. 2 sc in each sc (16 sc). Turn.

R5: Ch 1. 2 sc in each sc (32 sc). Turn.

R6: Ch 1. 2 sc in each sc (64 sc). Turn.

R7: Ch 1. 2 sc in each sc (128 sc). Change to B in last sc. Turn.

R8: Ch 1. 2 sc in each sc (256 sc). End. Cut string, leaving a long tail.

[1] Line up the edges of the plane and sew up using the tail of A. Weave in other A tail.

Tie the two B tails in an overhand knot. Slip onto the earring wire.

Make It Your Own

The string has terrific yardage and comes in a variety of colors. You could make a whole bunch of hyperbolic planes for Christmas ornaments.

Olive Love Bowl

A luscious skein of olive-colored yarn inspired this project. With its loosely single-spun thick-and-thin structure, I found it perfectly lovely and utterly impractical. Nonetheless, it jumped into my basket. A work of art in itself, it begged to become another work of art. I considered what to make with it. Its mere 68 yards would be chained up in no time, yielding maybe a trivet. I decided to approach it in another way: instead of crocheting the yarn itself, I crocheted it together with another, much thinner yarn. In quest of something to hold the yarn somewhat taut, I hit upon this technique of wrapping it around a *knitting loom* à la the string art popular in the '70s.

Skill level:
111

Yarn:
Rio De La Plata
Bulky (100% wool,
3.5 oz., 68 yd.),
1 ball Cull Gold-
Burgundy-Honey
Mustard 7 (A);
Euroflax Originals
(100% Linen, 50 g,
135 yd.), 1 skein
Sandalwood 18.44

Crochet hook:
D

Notions:
Tapestry needle
11½-inch knitting
loom

Finished size:
6 inches diameter by
3 inches tall

Gauge:
Varies.

Olive Love. Look at that yarn!

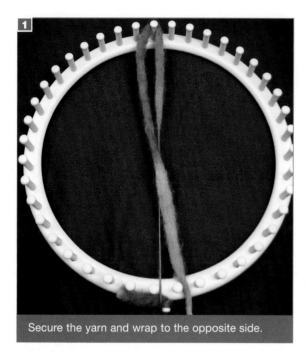

Secure the yarn and wrap to the opposite side.

A knitting loom is a round plastic tool with pegs. It is readily available at craft stores. Usually, a knitting loom is used for knitting without knitting needles—much like knitting with an old-fashioned spool knitter, but using a larger ring. It works by wrapping yarn around the pegs and then using a small awl to lift a loop over another loop. We'll be using it in a very different way!

1 Wrap A around pegs of loom: tie one end to the holding peg on the side of the loom. Wrap yarn counterclockwise around peg on opposite side.

When wrapping the yarn around the loom pegs, don't pull it too taut or it will tear. Just gently wrap it around the pegs with enough tension so it lies flat.

2 Wrap counterclockwise around the next peg on the opposite side.

3 Continue crossing and wrapping the yarn until loom is filled.

Continue wrapping yarn across loom.

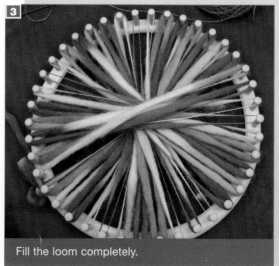

Fill the loom completely.

4. When the loom is full, turn it over so the pegs are underneath. With B underneath the loom, insert your hook in any space, about midway between the center and
5. the edge, and pull up a loop. Chain stitch around the yarn on the loom, being sure to chain around each strand.

Holding the loom "upside down" from its usual purpose allows you easier access for chaining.

You don't have to chain the strands in the order they're looped; some will overlap.
6. When is each strand is caught, work a second round about 1 inch toward the outside of the loom. Then pull the string through the final loop and cut, leaving enough tail to weave in.

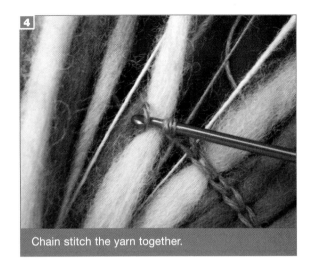

Chain stitch the yarn together.

Be sure to catch each strand in the first round.

Crochet a second round.

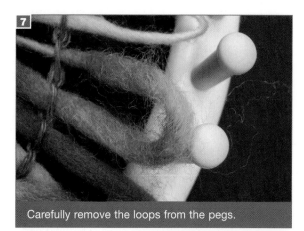
Carefully remove the loops from the pegs.

Rejoin B in any loop.

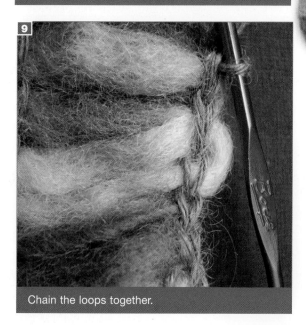
Chain the loops together.

7 To remove the work, carefully pull each loop off the pegs, keeping the work in its circular shape.

I chose to put the "straight stitch" side of the chain on the outside. You might want to put the "loop-stitch" side out.

8 Rejoin B in any outside loop.

Chain stitch the next loop and then the next, continuing around. (As you chain stitch, the bowl's top will pull in.) When you

9 chain the final loop, join to the first loop with chain stitch.

Weave in ends.

The finished bowl.

Make It Your Own

Looms come in different sizes, so use the one that works for you. Substitute any yarn that catches your fancy; a thick, lush yarn works best for this project. Try stranding the yarn in a different pattern—perhaps a flower pattern. You could even add beads for sparkle.

All Wrapped Up

As I wrote this book, I saved all the prototypes, false starts, and gauge swatches in a box. When I was done with all the projects, I dumped the box out. Here's what I found:

That's a big pile of stuff!

That big pile of stuff is my history of writing this book. Your own prototypes, false starts, and swatches (you *did* save them, didn't you?) make up your history of crocheting and reminds you of who you crochet for and why you crochet at all. All the parts are already made—you just have to piece them together in some way, much like patchwork.

This project allows you to shape your history into something real for the future. I can't tell you how to do it, because only you can create it. So one of these days, when you feel like you have enough stuff to have a conversation with it, dump it out. See what it tells you.

If it's very altruistic stuff, it might want to become an afghan for an elderly person in a nursing home or a batch of chemo caps. I'd be proud of that stuff. If it's very ooh-la-la, maybe it will be a shrug or wrap—something alive and exuberant. If it's sentimental, it might like to be in a shadow box, commemorating your first crochet or all the things you made for your family. (That would be a lovely display!) If it's practical, it will want to be a blanket

for winter. Or hats. Something warm and cozy. If it's very gregarious, it might like being sewn to the front of a card to give to a friend—maybe a fellow stitcher, maybe not. If you have enough stuff, it might be a bit of all those things.

My stuff, as it turns out, was not at all altruistic. No, no, it was very *ooh-la-la,* utterly impractical, unabashedly wild. It became an exuberant celebration of the exploration behind these designs.

May you enjoy making these projects— and making them your own—as much as I enjoyed creating them.

All Wrapped Up, from the front.

... and from the back.

Glossary

afghan stitch *See* Tunisian stitch.

blocking A method of evening out and shaping crocheted fabric. To steam block, hold a steam iron about 1 inch over the crochet fabric and mist (do not touch the iron to the fabric). Pin the piece to a board to given measurements, and let dry.

bobble A group of stitches worked in the same stitch in the bottom and joined at the top. The pattern tells you how many stitches to use in the bobble.

carabiner A device used by climbers to hook ropes to each other and to the rock. It makes a nifty attachment for bags, too.

carry (yarn) When changing colors or yarns and working just a few rows in the new color, don't cut the first color. Instead, just pick up the old color and rejoin at the new point.

chain (ch) The foundation for crochet, made by pulling a loop through the loop on the hook.

colorway Usually used to refer to multicolored yarn, this refers to the dominant color of the yarn. For instance, a yarn with red and pink and purple in it would be a red colorway.

crab stitch Also called reverse single crochet, this edging stitch is made by single crocheting from left to right.

craft board A board made of composite wood or cardboard usually with a grid of 1-inch blocks used to pin material to a given measurement.

crochet hook The tool used to loop a strand of yarn into fabric.

cluster A group of stitches worked in separate stitches at the bottom and joined at the top. The pattern tells you how many stitches to use in the cluster.

decrease (dec) To combine 2 stitches into 1.

ditch In rib stitch, this is the "valley" between the ridges of crochet.

fabric   In crochet, this refers to the material you make when you crochet.

felting   A method of shrinking the crocheted fabric—on purpose—by washing it in hot water. It makes the fabric denser.

freeform crochet   A technique of joining small motifs and/or crocheting random attachments in various yarns to create a tapestrylike fabric.

gauge   A measurement of the number of stitches and rows per inch. A gauge swatch can show whether the crocheter has the same tension that the pattern calls for. If the gauge is different, the finished object will be a different size. A swatch should be 4 inches by 4 inches to get a true measurement. If your swatch has more stitches than called for in the recommended gauge, try a smaller hook. If your swatch has fewer stitches than called for in the recommended gauge, try a larger hook.

granny square   A crochet motif made by working a series of shell stitches in the round and working extra shells at the corners to make it square. Traditionally, each round is in a different color.

in the round   Working crochet in a spiral rather than back and forth.

increase (inc)   To work 2 stitches in 1 single stitch. When working a circle, it's necessary to increase at given intervals so the circle increases in size without buckling.

knitting loom   A round plastic tool with pegs around its perimeter. Usually, a knitting loom is used for knitting without knitting needles, much like knitting with an old-fashioned spool knitter, but using a larger ring. You wrap yarn around the pegs and then use a small awl to lift a loop over another loop.

long stitch (or **spike stitch**)   To insert the hook 1 or more rows down, yarn over, and draw a loop through and up to level of the current row.

loop stitch   To insert your hook into a stitch as usual but then use your index finger of your free hand to form a loop about 1 inch long. Then you pick up both strands of the loop and draw them through. Wrap the yarn over your hook (as for a regular single crochet), and pull through all 3 loops on the hook.

LYS   Your local yarn store. If you don't know of a specialty yarn store near you (check your phone book or online), this could be the yarn section of a local craft and hobby store.

picot   A decorative edge made by chaining and then joining the chains with a slip stitch to form a little loop.

popcorn   To make a popcorn, work the given number of double crochets in the same stitch, remove the hook, reinsert it in the first stitch of the group, and hook the loop from the last stitch into the first stitch.

reverse single crochet   *See* crab stitch.

seaming   A way of attaching pieces of crocheted fabric.

scrumbling   *See* freeform crochet.

shell   A grouping of several stitches in 1 stitch. The pattern tells you how many stitches to put in the shell.

sliding loop   A way of starting a circle without leaving a hole. To do it, chain 2. Work stitches in the second chain from the hook and then pull the tail to tighten the hole.

slip knot   The small knot that begins a row of chain.

slip stitch (sl st)   The smallest stitch, used to scoot across the beginning of a row or to seam fabric together.

Tunisian stitch   Also called afghan stitch, this is a fusion of knit and crochet. Rather than working with 1 live stitch, you pick up stitches across the row and then work them off your hook. It makes a very sturdy fabric.

turning chain   The chain made at the beginning of a row to bring the yarn up to the height of the stitch.

woven stitch   To chain-1 and then single crochet across a row. On the second row, work the same pattern, putting single crochets in the space formed by the chain-1 on the previous row.

yarn over   To wrap the yarn over the hook from back to front.

Resources

Now that you're thoroughly hooked on crochet, you'll probably want to spend all your time crocheting and looking for new yarns to work with, new patterns to try, and all sorts of other things crochet-related. The following sections offer a few jumping-off points so you can get your crochet fix. Have fun!

Yarn

In your quest for yarn, supporting your local yarn shop (LYS) is always the best option. But sometimes you can't find the yarn you really, really want locally—or you can score a good deal online. Some of the projects in this book rely on specialty yarns made by these independent producers:

Sundara Yarns
sundarayarn.typepad.com
(Wrist Warmers, Chapter 8)
This one-woman operation based in Seattle produces hand-dyed sumptuous blends.

Araucania Nature Wool
(Table Runner, Chapter 5)
Made in Chile (www.araucaniayarns.com) distributed in United States by KFI (www.knittingfever.com), this yarn is available at some craft stores.

KnitPicks
PO Box 870760
Vancouver, WA 98687-7760
1-800-574-1323
knitpicks.com
(Maximal Mini Skirt, Chapter 7)
Find quality imported yarns here, including dye-your-own yarns in all weights, at crazy-low prices.

Jimmy Beans Wool
5000 Smithridge Drive
Reno, NV 89502
1-877-532-3891
www.jimmybeanswool.com
(Sleep Glasses, Chapter 11)
If you can't find it at your LYS, check the wide assortment of yarns here.

Shangri-La Crafts
3392 Adeline Street
Berkeley, CA 94709
510-601-5100
info@shangri-lacrafts.com
www.shangri-lacrafts.com/silkyarn.html
(Bird Nest Bowl, Chapter 5)
You can find several grades of recycled silk yarns here.

Books

A crochet stitch guide can help you explore your *crochet-tivity*. I've listed guides I consult in creating my designs. To find your own favorite book, go to your local bookstore and flip through their offerings until you find the one that has directions that make sense to you.

Barnden, Betty. *The Crochet Stitch Bible*. Iola, WI: Krause Publications, 2004.

Chan, Doris. *Amazing Crochet Lace: New Fashions Inspired by Old-Fashioned Lace*. New York: Potter Craft, 2006.

Christmas, Carolyn. *101 Easy Tunisian Stitches*. Berne, IN: DRG/Annie's Attic, 2004.

Eckman, Edie. *The Crochet Answer Book*. North Adams, MA: Storey, 2005.

Kooler, Donna. *Encyclopedia of Crochet*. Little Rock, AK: Leisure Arts, 2002.

Levyhamburg, Deborah, *101 Double-Ended Hook Stitches: Crochet*. Berne, IN: DRG/Annie's Attic, 2002.

Norton, Carol. *Tapestry Crochet*. Loveland, CO: Interweave Press, 1991.

Reader's Digest. *The Ultimate Sourcebook of Knitting and Crochet Stitches*. Pleasantville, NY: Collins & Brown, 2003.

Online

These sites are good, solid resources for learning about crochet:

craftyarncouncil.com
Site of the Craft Yarn Council of America

www.crochet.org
Site of the Crochet Guild of America

The following sites take you beyond, into the realm of freeform crochet, creative sculpture, and more.

Crochetme.com
Hip crochet patterns and smart techniques.

crochet.nu/index.html
Go here to learn all about scrumbling and freeform crochet.

www.knotjustknitting.com
Check out Prudence Mapstone's creative blending of freeform crochet and knitting.

www.crochetlab.com
This funky, independent site is self-described as "an eclectic compendium of crochet-related stuff" that will definitely stretch your brain fibers.

www.crochetpatterncentral.com/ directory/tunisian_crochet.php
This site is pattern central for a variety of projects in Tunisian crochet.

Simple guides
to better
crafts!

THE COMPLETE **IDIOT'S GUIDE** TO

32 pages of full-color photographs

Knitting & Crocheting
THIRD EDITION
Illustrated

Keep your stitches straight with hundreds of step-by-step photos and illustrations

Barbara Breiter and Gail Diven

ISBN: 978-1-59257-491-9

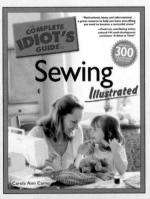